W9-BNI-108

inside your customer's imagination

ALSO BY CHIP R. BELL

Kaleidoscope: Delivering Innovative Service That Sparkles

Sprinkles: Creating Awesome Experiences through Innovative Service

The 9½ Principles of Innovative Service

Wired and Dangerous: How Your Customers Have Changed and What to Do about It (with John R. Patterson)

Take Their Breath Away: How Imaginative Service Creates Devoted Customers (with John R. Patterson)

Customer Loyalty Guaranteed: Create, Lead, and Sustain Remarkable Customer Service (with John R. Patterson)

Magnetic Service: Secrets for Creating Passionately Devoted Customers (with Bilijack R. Bell)

Service Magic: The Art of Amazing Your Customers (with Ron Zemke)

Dance Lessons: Six Steps to Great Partnerships in Business & Life (with Heather Shea)

Customers as Partners: Building Relationships That Last

Managing Knock Your Socks Off Service (with Ron Zemke)

inside your customer's imagination

5 Secrets for Creating Breakthrough Products, Services, and Solutions

Chip R. Bell

Bestselling author of *Customers As Partners*

Berrett–Koehler Publishers, Inc.

Berrett-Koehler Publishers, Inc.
1333 Broadway, Suite 1000
Oakland, CA 94612-1921
Tel: (510) 817-2277
Fax: (510) 817-2278
www.bkconnection.com

ORDERING INFORMATION

Quantity sales. Special discounts are available on quantity purchases by corporations, associations, and others. For details, contact the "Special Sales Department" at the Berrett-Koehler address above.

Individual sales. Berrett-Koehler publications are available through most bookstores. They can also be ordered directly from Berrett-Koehler: Tel: (800) 929-2929; Fax: (802) 864-7626; www.bkconnection.com.

Orders for college textbook / course adoption use. Please contact Berrett-Koehler: Tel: (800) 929-2929; Fax: (802) 864-7626.

Distributed to the U.S. trade and internationally by Penguin Random House Publisher Services.

Printed in Canada

Berrett-Koehler books are printed on long-lasting acid-free paper. When it is available, we choose paper that has been manufactured by environmentally responsible processes. These may include using trees grown in sustainable forests, incorporating recycled paper, minimizing chlorine in bleaching, or recycling the energy produced at the paper mill.

Library of Congress Cataloging-in-Publication Data
Names: Bell, Chip R., author.
Title: Inside your customer's imagination : 5 secrets for creating
breakthrough products, services, and solutions / Chip R. Bell.
Description: First edition. | Oakland, CA : Berrett-Koehler Publishers,
[2020] | Includes bibliographical references and index.
Identifiers: LCCN 2020012741 | ISBN 9781523090204 (hardcover ; alk. paper)
| ISBN 9781523090211 (pdf) | ISBN 9781523090228 (epub)
Subjects: LCSH: Customer services. | Customer relations. | New products.
Classification: LCC HF5415.5 .B4345 2020 | DDC 658.8/343—dc23
LC record available at https://lccn.loc.gov/2020012741

First Edition
27 26 25 24 23 22 21 20 10 9 8 7 6 5 4 3 2 1

Interior designer and book producer: Happenstance Type-O-Rama
Cover designer: Susan Malikowski, DesignLeaf Studio
Cover photos: Leigh Lofgren. The dunk mug was designed by Dominic Skinner for Mocha UK.
Interior illustration: Happenstance Type-O-Rama

To Nancy

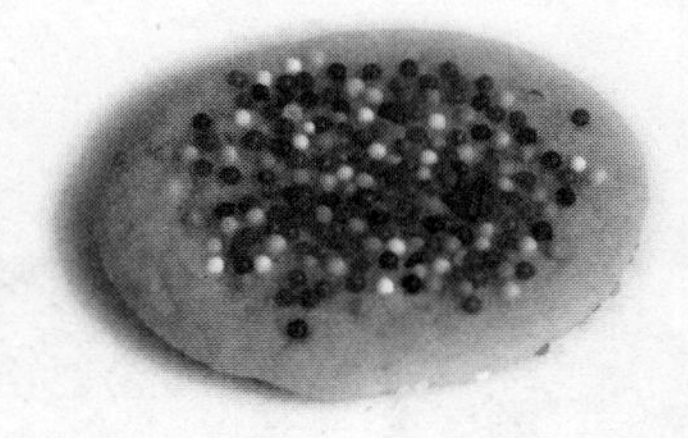

Dominic Skinner sat in a coffee shop in Surrey, England, with his sketch pad and hot tea. He overheard a customer at a nearby table commenting to a friend on how great it would be if their hot tea cups could warm their cookies. From inside the customer's imagination, Dominic fashioned the breakthrough cup pictured on the book cover and here on this page, and he sold the idea to Mocha UK. This book is dedicated to all who partner with the ingenuity of their customers to create breakthrough products, services, and solutions.

Contents

Secret 4 ✷ Trust

Secret 5 ✷ Passion

Beginning the Adventure

The Iraq Museum in Baghdad contains a stone that displays a carved ninth-century BC relief of Assyrian King Shalmaneser III shaking hands with Babylonian King Marduk Zakir Shumi. Shalmaneser ruled Assyria (now Iraq and Turkey) for over thirty-five years. Two features of the relief are worth noting. It is the first picture discovered of two people shaking hands. And each man is carrying a shepherd's staff, believed to be a mark of royal authority on peaceful occasions.

The handshake has been the symbol for partnership for almost three thousand years. Some historians believe it became a trusted gesture of alliances because the open hands revealed no weapons; the up and down motion was intended to shake out any weapons hidden in a sleeve. It is associated with a pledge or promise.

A partnership is the paramount confederation for creating and nurturing innovation. If you examine the cultural components of organizations famous for innovation, you will see that they are filled with partnership virtues—curiosity, purpose, growth, and trust. Most innovative enterprises have successfully exorcised fear from their workplaces. Most have elevated passion and erased protectionism. Most revere organizational forms that support freedom and creativity over control, rigidity, and judgment.

Organizations today ardently pursue innovation because simply continuously improving their offerings is not sufficient to remain competitive. However, most organizations that are thriving today have already been reorganized, Leaned, and Six Sigmaed to the max. Additionally, successful disruptors are strongly influencing their "go to market" strategy. The dilemma facing most enterprises is illustrated by the following story.

The CEO of a small company was meeting with her direct reports at their weekly gathering. "How can we increase our company's performance by 10 percent?" she asked the group. The energized audience began brainstorming ways to cut costs, boost sales, reduce waste, and tighten expenses. In the middle of their spirited ideation, she stopped them. "Let me ask a different question. How can we increase it by 100 percent?" The room was silent for a minute. Finally, the COO said, "You can't get there from here. We would have to completely reinvent how we perform." Such is the reality of today's business world.

But there is more to the ninth-century relief than a handshake between kings. There is the symbol of a shepherd's crook, a long staff used to protect and guide sheep. The shepherd has always been a symbol of courage, one who protected sheep against wild animals. Through the ages, the shepherd has symbolized calm and safety. Shepherding a partnership implies the parties take great care of one another; it also suggests taking great care of the relationship itself. The king of Assyria and the king of Babylonia announced an innovative partnership with that handshake.

Enter a new player on the innovation partnership scene: the customer. This "other king" has been historically treated as a bit player. It can sound like "We know our customers and what is best for them" or "You don't understand how we do business here" or "Customers in the boardroom? Are you joking? What about insider information and airing our dirty laundry?" Some organizations claim a partnership with customers, but when the relationship is put under a microscope, the "other king" is merely a "member of the court."

While the customer is the focal point of this book, the definition of "customer" is broad. I define it as the person (or people) who is the target of your offering. That means it could be a vendor at the loading dock. It could be an external supplier or expert advisor. And it could be an employee to whom you provide leadership, coaching, and support. We all have people we serve. This book is also about encounters with customers that rely on a relationship, not just an encounter with a chatbot, robot, or programmed message. It provides the practices and perspectives to help a person, a unit, or an organization serve in ways that deepen relationships, encourage their longevity, and maximize their creative potential.

When organizations attempt to create a product or service they hope the customer will buy or they craft a solution they hope the customer will accept, the creating and crafting are typically done with a factory mentality. That means raw materials, expertise, and ideas are assembled in a protected environment far from the ultimate users and then sold to them in the marketplace. Although market data is gathered (so that we can make what customers will want), the customer is never invited into the "factory" to assist. That mentality can fuel a separateness and an air of superiority. Sure, there are test markets, pilots, and prototypes. But the customer is never the "other king." And the shepherd's staff is not a tool to protect the relationship.

"The purpose of business is to create and keep a customer," wrote Peter Drucker, the father of modern management.[1] Organizations create a customer by convincing a prospect that the enterprise is uniquely qualified to meet her or his needs and expectations through their offerings. Assuming that offering continues to do its job for the customer, that customer is kept through ongoing positive experiences with the organization.

This truism is based on two assumptions—the customer knows his or her needs, and the organization has offerings in sync with them. It is, therefore, an equation grounded in a certain degree of certainty. But what if the customer's needs are emerging or vague, or even unknown? What if they start out definite but become imprecise? What if their needs do not closely match the organization's offerings?

Historically, this vagueness on either side of the equation would trigger a few scenarios. The customer would settle for an offering thought to be not wholly satisfactory but would say, "It was the best I could find." The customer would not settle for an offering that was slightly off and would continue the search. The organization would try to get the customer to buy something it already had to offer that would only partially meet the customer's needs. Or the organization would suggest the customer continue the search.

But what would happen if the customer were so loyal to the organization he or she was willing to hang in there at the juncture between need and offering until it all became clearer? What would be the outcome if the organization were so loyal to the customer it was willing to help the customer discover the solution, including one it did not offer? What if customer and organization could meet at that need-offering juncture and together figure out an outcome that was entirely new? Envision what the path would be if the best answer lay inside the imagination of the customer.

The book you are reading is about creating a partnership between "kings with staffs." Its complexion is one that helps the parties involved source and share the very best of their imaginations. A partnership is a marriage of equals with common goals and mutual values but different talents and resources. That marriage works when both are treated as kings and the shepherding role is assumed by all. In the process, the loyalty of each deepens as their collective achievement increases.

Chip

Lake Oconee, Georgia
June 2020

Introduction

WELCOME TO YOUR CUSTOMER'S IMAGINATION

Imagination is a place where all
the important answers live.
—JOE MENO

We are not actually there yet. But it is nearby. Your customer will have to invite you in. That will likely happen later on. At this point, I am merely preparing you for the journey ahead and letting you know what you might expect. There will be special provisions involved, but we can talk about those later. First, we will explore why we are here. A thorough understanding of the rationale is important, so this will not be a drive-by explanation.

Let's start with a map of your journey ahead. Organizations need breakthrough products, services, and solutions to compete effectively. They need the customer's imagination to ensure the discovery of innovative and valued offerings. Accessing the customer's imagination requires a co-creation partnership that invites and attracts creative contributions.

A co-creation partnership takes 1) curiosity that uncovers insight, 2) grounding that promotes clear focus, 3) discovery that fosters risk-taking, 4) trust that safeguards partnership purity, and 5) passion that inspires energized generosity. This journey leads to ingenious outcomes and a customer who emerges as an advocate.

Now let's slow down and unpack the parts of this map with a bit more detail. Innovation is all about new. In fact, the word itself comes from its root, *nova*. The word has also come to mean unique, novel, and ingenious. Innovation today is a big deal to all organizations. They ardently pursue innovation because simply improving their offerings (products, services, or solutions) is not enough to remain competitive. Their boards, owners, and stakeholders continually encourage them to stay on the cutting edge. Customers also want new, not just the same old same old.

Organizations typically turn to their research and development departments for assistance with innovation. They visit other companies to learn best practices they can emulate. They offer incentives to employees to provide suggestions and ideas. They create innovation centers and design test labs. All this innovating is aimed at creating offerings that will hopefully meet their prospects' or customers' needs and be valued.

Innovating offerings that will meet customers' needs assumes those needs are known. But in the fast-paced, ever-changing world of commerce, customers don't always know what they want. They might have a hunch but not a concrete or complete definition. No one asked for a fax machine, a laptop computer, an answering machine, or even a bicycle, but customers valued the benefits these products provided. Henry Ford reportedly said, "If I had given customers what they wanted, I would have given them faster horses."

Consider what the journey with the customer would be if you understood the customer's needs so deeply you were assured of absolutely nailing a match. What if you ran the innovating approach of most companies completely backward, starting with the customer, instead of with a hoped-for solution? How would it be if you involved customers in such a manner that their hopes and aspirations were revealed, to them and to you? This is the venue where customers are treated as true partners.

A partnership can be a key to accessing the customer's imagination. Done properly, it is an alliance of trust and a liaison of equality. But most organizations manage customer partnerships in a way that the customer, if a partner at all, is more of a junior partner. The organization remains in charge and lets the customer have a limited role. It's like plowing with my dad when I was a kid.

When I was seven or eight years old, I would sit with my dad in the tractor seat as together we plowed a field. We were partners. But when we came to the end of the row, he took over. He raised the plow, slowed the tractor, made the turn, lined the tractor up on the next row, and lowered the plow for me to resume steering. I felt like a partner, but I was clearly not an equal partner, only an active participant. It was an appropriate status since I was too short to reach the tractor pedals. The customer, on the other hand, is plenty tall.

What This Book Is About . . . and Not About

Customer participation is not a new concept. There are many examples of customers being encouraged to get involved. The Craddock Terry Hotel, housed in a 1905 converted shoe factory in Lynchburg, Virginia, invites guests to take the hotel's dog concierge, Penny Loafer, on a walk through the town's historical district, and to "decorate your own tree" during the winter holidays with shoe-themed ornaments. Vans shoes enthusiasts have been able to design their own kicks since Vans's first week of operation, when the company's founder told a customer to go to a fabric store and buy cloth in the brighter color she wanted.[1] Two of Starbucks's most popular items—cake pops and pumpkin spice lattes—came from the imagination of their customers. So did splash sticks and free Wi-Fi, along with 150,000 other innovations via the company's My Starbucks Idea platform.[2] Participation helps customers put skin in the game.

But participation and partnership are not the same thing. The focus of this book is co-creation, on getting customers fully integrated into the creation process, not just tangentially or superficially invited to participate. Dell computers had co-creation hardwired into its DNA from the start. Michael Dell, from his dorm room at the University of Texas, started selling computer upgrade kits. He got a license as a vendor, giving him access to discounted parts, and sold assembled computers to customers at an economy price. The seventy-billion-dollar company today continues to actively involve customers in design. Customer answers to "What would you really want this thing to do? Is there a different way to accomplish that?" type of questions get turned into offerings, created *by* customers, not just *for* customers. Michael Dell himself visits chats rooms, not as the CEO, but as an anonymous, caring partner. What they learn enables quick turnaround when mistakes occur.

Here is another way to consider the difference. When businesses are asked why they do what they do, they acknowledge they are in the business of creating products, providing services, and crafting solutions for customers. If that purpose is done well, they keep score by generating a profit and/or growing. The operative word is *for*. This book is about creating that same outcome, only it is performed *with* customers, not just on their behalf.

The word "customerization" was introduced by management guru Tom Peters in his 1992 book *Liberation Management*. "Customer focus," he wrote, "still clutches the tired imagery of 'us' designing to attend to 'them'; 'us' as active, 'they' as passive."[3] It is a Copernicus-like view, with the customer revolving around the products, services, or solutions provider. His metaphor suggested a better approach: to think of the relationship as being like the one between a potter and potter's wheel, where the provider supplies the clay and the machinery and the customer creates the pot—"something neither one could have accomplished alone." But let us be clear on who is the customer.

Labels are always imprecise. Earlier the word "customer" was used to mean someone with a need and an expectation. He or she might go by a multitude of monikers, including client, patient, guest, colleague, student, citizen, patron, member, consumer, or partner. We will call them all customers—those with a need seeking some individual or entity to help meet that need.

When a company creates a product to be sold to a customer, they might be labeled a manufacturer, builder, supplier, or producer at the wholesale level, a merchant, seller, or dealer at the retail end of the marketplace supply chain. When a company delivers a service to a customer, they might be called a service provider, and if their stock in trade is expertise or advice, like a doctor or lawyer, they might be known as a professional services provider. Since all are providing a tangible or an intangible supply of something of value to a customer, we will refer to them all as a "provider." It is not a term of exactness, only one of convenience.

This book is focused on interpersonal encounters between customers and human providers. The settings for meeting customer needs can be anywhere and anytime. These might be face to face, ear to ear, or even click to click, but they are not AI or robot to customer, at least not in the foreseeable future!

Finally, an important assumption. Imagination might be unlimited but business practices are not. This book does not suggest abandoning fiscal responsibility, reasonable capacity, or organizational values. It is important for partners in all relationships to be generous, but not sacrificial.

Inside Your Customer's Imagination—A Sneak Peek

Deep inside every customer is a treasure trove of half-baked ideas, creative capacity, and ingenuity-in-the-raw. Some customers are aware that trove exists; others have no clue. The key to unlocking this vessel of innovative goodies resides only with the customer. Think of the challenge as a bit like helping a very cautious person demonstrate courage. When an organization builds that kind of deep, valued partnership with customers—a coalition laced with curiosity, grounding, discovery, trust, and passion—three important outcomes occur.

First, some customers discover their treasure chest. Second, some customers become willing to open that chest and share it with the provider. But a third thing happens that is purely magical. It changes the provider as well, and the entire relationship is enriched. The value of the co-created offering becomes more valuable to all involved, ensuring the long-term future of the partnership. There are partnerships with customers. And then there are co-creation partnerships. Co-creation partnerships operate with intimate customer connections, a high level of structural freedom, and an obsession with "being the customer." Inclusion and transparency are second nature.

Co-creation partnerships are those in which all parties relinquish any effort to control or manipulate the outcome. They are populated by people putting all effort into being entirely authentic and real. They are devoted to discovery and learning, not dedicated to convincing. We all wear masks, in part to protect ourselves against rejection. When a provider is completely genuine in front of a customer, it changes the nature of the relationship from cautious to unguarded. Energy typically devoted to cover and protection becomes available for insight and discovery.

Co-creation partnerships value candor without rancor. Providers in these relationships are assertively candid, with the intention of helping, not hurting, the customer. There is a cleanness in such relationships in which the value of straightforward interaction is unmistakable. Great providers care enough to be forthright; they are also curious and learning oriented enough to invite and accept frankness from their customers. Partnering is always a two-way relationship.

Co-creation partnerships are connections filled with zeal and obvious attention to the customer's need, issue, problem, or concern. It is the "be all . . . there" feature of undivided and uninterrupted focus on what matters most to the customer. When customers sense a provider is passionate about championing their cause and finding a novel solution, they are more willing to open up their imagination and meld it with the provider's imagination for an ingenious synergistic outcome that is often labeled a breakthrough.

Five Secrets for Co-Creation Partnerships

DHL is the FedEx and UPS of Europe. With over a half million employees, they are the largest private carrier in the world. Their commitment to co-creation partnerships takes many forms, including their annual DHL Innovation Days. Customers and business partners connect in an inspirational atmosphere to think outside the box and honor creative minds with the DHL Innovation Awards. When customers wanted help rethinking supply chains and logistics to improve future business performance, DHL created a series of intensive hands-on workshops that brought together DHL experts with customers to do scenario planning for future applications. It yielded breakthroughs like Parcelcopter, a drone delivery project; smart glasses, an augmented reality that improved warehouse picking efficiency by 25 percent; and "Maintenance on Demand," co-created with DHL customer Volvo Trucks, which uses sensors to automatically send back vehicle performance data to identify when and where truck maintenance will be needed.[4]

In the pages to come, we will delve deeply into the five tactics—I call them secrets (figure 1)—for creating and sustaining a co-creation partnership. Their foundation comes from the components of all renowned innovation companies, cultures, and relationships. The goal is to encourage customers to discover and disclose their imagination and meld it with the provider's imagination in order to create an offering that exactly matches the customer's hopes and aspirations. Along the way, we will explore techniques for applying these secrets in real-world situations.

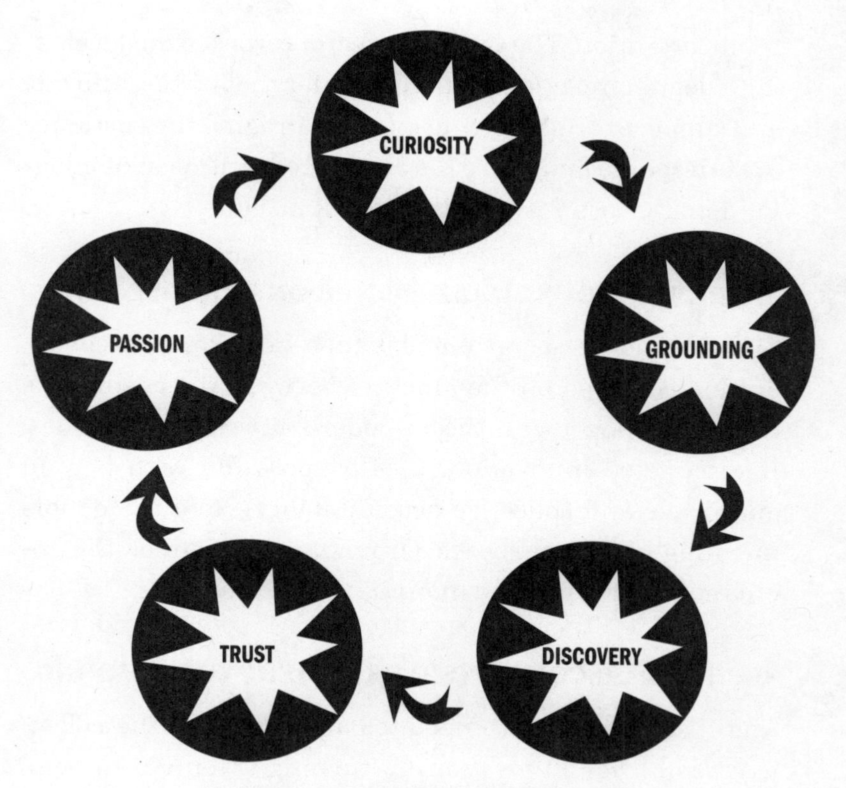

FIGURE 1. Co-creation partnership secrets

When you watch a video of an Olympic athletic performance in slow motion, you see the sterile mechanics. But when you see the performance live, you experience something almost supernatural. The magic of a co-creation partnership is the confluence of actions, attitudes, and associations that comes from these five building blocks or tactics.

SECRET 1. CURIOSITY: BE THE CUSTOMER

"Be the customer" borrows from the "be the ball" advice coaches give young athletes to encourage them to focus and retain attention. The Curiosity secret zeroes in on developing a deep connection with a customer that bonds, affirms, and supports, thus inviting and encouraging the customer to both source and share his or her treasure chest of imagination. Curiosity is the extractor of insight.

SECRET 2. GROUNDING: PARTNER ON PURPOSE

The Grounding secret enables high-performance collaboration centered on the juncture between the customer's needs and hopes and the provider's mission and values. It is targeted innovation. It is purpose-full with helpful guardrails and collective accountability. Note the double meaning of "on purpose." Grounding disciplines the co-creation partnership to maintain a clear focus.

SECRET 3. DISCOVERY: SPARK DAREDEVIL LEARNING

The Discovery secret expedites and catalyzes the collective search for innovation by turning tryouts into bold, risk-taking learning adventures. It engenders growth on steroids, learning that is empowering and aha producing. And it provides a welcoming portal for the customer's imagination to emerge from inside out. Discovery fosters risk-taking and experimentation.

SECRET 4. TRUST: PURSUE TRUTH, JUSTICE, AND THE IMAGINATION WAY

The Trust secret centers on being an active custodian of the relationship so that it always honors candor, respects clear work agreements, and has planned for the inevitable hiccups likely to be a part of a vibrant, high-energy partnership. It harnesses creativity as it guides its transformation from rough idea to polished execution. Trust safeguards the co-creation partnership to preserve its purity and wholesomeness.

SECRET 5. PASSION: NEVER STOP COURTING

The Passion secret fuels the co-creation partnership with signs of admiration and actions of caring that keep the alliance fresh and spirited. As an obvious source of focused joy, abundance, and gratitude, it makes a co-creation partnership contagious, motivating others to support it and inspiring them to emulate it. Passion sparks energized generosity.

Making the shift from viewing customers as junior partners to full partners requires actions that convince and consistency that proves. Customers are not accustomed to being in an equal position with providers. The whole negotiation of price, for example, illustrates the challenge of partnering in today's competitive, transaction-driven world of commerce. The traditional view of "You have a need, I fill it" must be converted to use "we" pronouns.

Co-Creation Is beyond Customer-Centric

Countless business books today focus on the pinnacle of a provider-to-customer relationship as being one that is customer-centric. (Whether B2C or B2B, all business relationships are P2P—people to people.) Their view zeroes in on the right side of a four-point continuum that runs from customer hostile (we all can name a few of those) to customer aware, customer friendly, and customer-centric. But there is another, higher plane, one underutilized in today's "hunt for breakthroughs" world (figure 2).

CUSTOMER HOSTILE	CUSTOMER AWARE	CUSTOMER FRIENDLY	CUSTOMER-CENTRIC	CO-CREATION PARTNERSHIPS

FIGURE 2. Provider-to-customer relationship continuum

Customer aware organizations are characterized by customer accommodation rather than support. *Customer friendly* organizations give enough lip service to customer service that it shows up in pockets of their service delivery, but not consistently.

To say a provider is *customer-centric* generally means it is keeping the customer at the forefront of thinking, planning, and decision making.

Co-creation partnerships are about keeping the customer present and in the driver's seat along with the provider, so the customer becomes much more than just the recipient of a provider executing with the customer in mind. As explained in this book, it features an approach more like a potluck "dinner on the grounds" right after church. People love it because everyone contributes to the meal. The salads at the beginning of the buffet line are just as important as the cakes at the end. Its power lies in the fact that it is co-created, not just customer-centric.

A Look Ahead: Curiosity

What does a provider need to do to encourage a customer to enter into a relationship that makes innovation far more likely? We start with curiosity since it establishes the rapport and lays the foundation for the trust your customer needs to reveal their imagination and join you in the creation of a novel offering that precisely meets their needs, expectations, hopes, and aspirations. Curiosity is conveyed through eccentric listening, witnessing like an anthropologist, and inquiring in a way that is unleashed (bold) and unfiltered (without bias). Pay close attention to the partnering crib notes at the end of each chapter. They will provide a thumbnail sketch of key takeaways to practice and master.

Partnership is a verb disguised as a noun.
It is a force released, "un-nouned," when
dreams connect and service is gracefully given.[5]

—FROM *CUSTOMERS AS PARTNERS*

Secret 1

CURIOSITY

Be the Customer

Curiosity is the very basis of education
and if you tell me that curiosity killed the cat,
I say only the cat died nobly.

—ARNOLD EDINBOROUGH

Carl Rogers had an eccentric curiosity. He and I had lunch at a restaurant near the beach at La Jolla, California, where he lived and worked at the Center for the Studies of the Person. It was the early 1980s; Dr. Rogers was considered one of the most renowned psychologists on the planet. We were strangers as the salad was served; we were intimate friends by the time the waiter brought the check. Between courses, he was charmingly open, wonderfully authentic, and as warmhearted as a kitten.

"You are the oldest?" he asked. When I nodded in the affirmative, he said, "I was the middle child of six; I sometimes felt insignificant. What does 'oldest' feel like?" We had just started the appetizer and I already felt I was with an old friend who needed me. His queries were random, asymmetrical, sometimes out of left field, yet always with the reciprocity of a mirror. He did not interview; we explored with the casualness and cordiality of a conversation about a book or movie we both enjoyed. His curiosity was exhilarating, valuable, and new. The conversation felt like wandering in a magical forest rather than staying up on the main road.

Together We Uncover Insight

Curiosity is fundamentally an optimistic treasure hunt—a gallant search that occurs without proof or guarantee. Curiosity is a human itch in search of a scratch. It reflects a yearning to know, not in a pious or smug way, but rather like the resolution of emotional dissonance—a familiar tune that stops before the last bar. Curiosity may have been death to the cat, but it is the birthplace of ideas. And it is a static state, like hunger, desire, or affinity, until it is activated. Curiosity in action feeds the yearning. We start here because curiosity is the secret map to accessing and mining your customer's imagination.

Curiosity shows up in three ways: eccentric listening, anthropological witnessing, and unleashed and unfiltered inquiry (figure 3). "Eccentric" means off center or from a unique angle, like my conversation with Dr. Rogers; "anthropological" suggests viewing with the heart of a social anthropologist who seeks to interpret, not evaluate; and "unleashed" (i.e., assertive or bold) and "unfiltered" (i.e., without bias or defense) suggest an authentic search rather than a fair weather one.

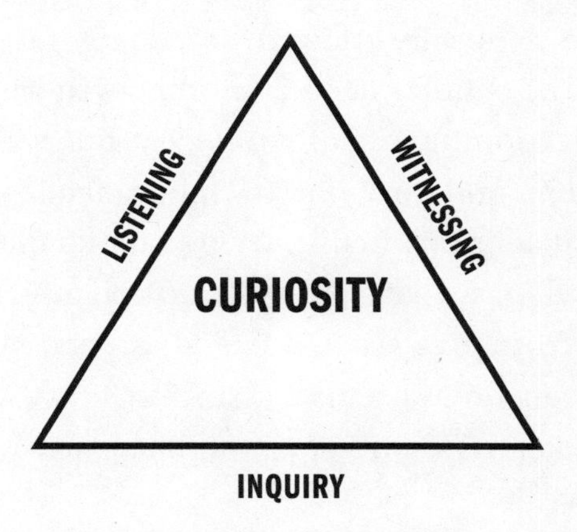

FIGURE 3. Curiosity revealed

The function of eccentric listening in innovation is to be a catalyst to insight, not just understanding. Insight is the "aha" we get when the "why" is revealed, not just the "what," when implication and appreciation are surfaced, not simply comprehension. We can half-listen our way to a superficial understanding. But eccentric listening positions a relationship to operate more on the plane of unending mental lights turning on. While obviously enriching the relationship, it also helps scaffold a performance stage for an alliance of innovation.

The practice of curiosity also requires assertive witness to the customer's world much as an anthropologist eagerly seeks to understand a culture without letting an egocentric or ethnocentric orientation shape a judgment. It is the pursuit of something potentially very valuable and, as such, much like a treasure hunt. It entails watching the customer in action; gaining deep knowledge of the customer's setting; and reading the norms, customs, emotional cues, and guideposts that shape customer attitudes and behaviors.

Inquiry is generally viewed as asking for information. However, in the context of co-creation partnering, it is much more. It is questioning to confirm clarity, querying to increase understanding, and probing to solicit feedback. Franklin P. Jones comically put his finger on the challenge of genuine inquiry when he said, "Honest criticism is hard to take, particularly from a relative, a friend, an acquaintance, or a stranger." Groucho Marx had a similar witty view: "People say I don't take criticism very well, but I say, 'What the hell do they know?'"

The opposite of curiosity is not indifference. The opposite is a judgmental orientation to life. People without curiosity tend to be opinionated, hypercritical, and obstinate in their views. They often scrutinize their world in absolutes, not with a sense of humility and wonderment. They are reticent to change and defensive of their positions. All these features are detriments to innovation since they are closed to newness and change.

Curiosity takes pacing the provider-customer dialogue so its ebb and flow is not governed by interest (which is omnipresent) but rather by the collective and mutual desires of the parties involved. It is an exchange that facilitates passion, kindles free thinking, and shuns judgments that retard, rebuke, or restrain. In a word, it is welcoming. An egalitarian playground, its dynamism and inventiveness invite serendipity and champion whimsy.

What follows are three chapters designed to more deeply examine perspectives, practices, and tools valuable in applying curiosity to customer hopes and aspirations for an innovative outcome.

CHAPTER 1

Practice Eccentric Listening

Listening is a magnetic and strange thing, a creative force. The friends who listen to us are the ones we move toward. When we are listened to, it creates us, makes us unfold and expand.

—KARL A. MENNINGER

"But you aren't listening to me!" The words ricocheted out of the conference room and down the hall, seeping into every cubicle on the floor. And it tactlessly lassoed everyone in ear-shot into involuntary eavesdropping.

"What do you mean?" the other side of the confrontation responded in his own defense. "I have been listening to you throughout our whole meeting." It was a design meeting between an engineer and a key customer. The decibel level of their contest suddenly went hushed and died after the next heart-splitting line.

"You might be listening to me talk, but you're not getting what I say!"

Organizations in search of innovation with customers brag about their commitment to great customer listening.

Some show off their industrial-strength survey research with its heavy-duty statistics. Others boast about how often their executives talk to a customer or sit behind one-way glass at a focus group. "We are focused heavily these days on big data," one executive bragged to another. The retort she received from her colleague: "What about *real* data? The kind you get from listening?"

Curiosity in action comes in many forms, depending on the pursuit. Archaeologists gratify their curiosity with a pick, shovel, magnifying glass, and brush. Innovating with customers is the hunt for a novel product, service, or solution. The bridge between curiosity and discovery is collective insight. And we unleash insight through deep understanding acquired through listening, observing, and inquiring. This chapter focuses on a special level of listening—eccentric, as in unique, odd, unstructured, artistic, emotional, and fluid.

Meanwhile, back at that conference room, the lament of the customer was for recordings on the heart, not for sound waves on the ear. The customer did not feel understood and therefore did not feel esteemed. Today's customers feel over-surveyed and undervalued. Too much effort goes into listening to customers talk rather than valuing what is said (or not said) and, more importantly, meant (or implied). Too often, the pursuit is for facts rather than feelings, conversation instead of candor.

Start with Empathy

Empathy starts with simply attentively listening while asking yourself: "What must my customer be feeling right now? How might I feel if our roles were reversed?" Empathy begins by caring enough to give undivided attention. Think about what "undivided" really means—not broken into parts. Empathy is enhanced through a reflective response. Receptivity to the customer's feelings enables you to provide a tailor-made reflective response that says, "I've been there as well." This gesture, another way of saying "I am similar to you," promotes the kinship and closeness vital to customer trust.

Reflective responses can be a short personal story that lets your customer know you appreciate his or her feelings. Mildly self-deprecating anecdotes can work well, too. Above all, empathy is best served laced with humility and sensitivity. Think of it as the emotional countenance of a parent soothing a child awakened by a nightmare. And it is blended with authenticity. If you feel awkward, say you do. If you feel excited, say so. The sooner you speak your feelings, the faster your customer will match your vulnerability, propelling you on the path to trust.

Eccentric listening is like listening to a creative child tell a story.
The storyline is curved and rambling, rarely straight;
the insight is hidden, rarely in plain view.

Instead of listening to understand, focus on listening to interpret. Pretend you are an emotional translator, not just an eavesdropper. Paraphrasing is an interpersonal tool that involves listeners mirroring the meaning of what was heard as a sentence that ends in a period, not a question mark or an exclamation point. It is not parroting or repeating, which can sound wooden; it is your words reflecting the meaning you heard. But the greatest gain comes in the attentiveness required to paraphrase in the first place. With practice, it will stop feeling contrived and become as natural and as effective as master paraphrasers Oprah Winfrey, Howard Stern, or Ellen DeGeneres.

Co-creation partnerships are not about a love affair. Yet they possess some of the same features as being in love. Recall the early days with a person with whom you were in love. You hung on to their every word, did not miss a single nonverbal, and were attentive to their every whim. Your antenna of adoration was raised high, and you looked hard for tiny, subtle ways to emotionally connect. That is what empathy looks like in action. Its magic is in its capacity to cause its target to lower their emotional shield and model your openness.

EDiS Company is a highly successful building solutions firm headquartered in Wilmington, Delaware. A number of years ago they unexpectedly lost an important client. It was a wakeup call. After doing some customer forensics work to unravel the root cause of his sudden departure, they learned there had been interpersonal signals they missed that could have warned them of his exit in time to turn the relationship around. CEO Brian DiSabatino had always insisted on a mid-project review with EDiS's clients. Armed with this new insight, he wisely added questions aimed at the interpersonal relationship, not just the project, to their Compass review. "The byproduct of this addition," said DiSabatino, "was it created a stronger partnership with our clients enabling them to offer creative ideas we still had time to implement and stay within the scope of the bid and project plan."

Be the Customer

My business partner John Patterson and I were asked by a large wholesale auto auction company to help them understand the process exporters used to purchase a vehicle at the auction and then get it to dealers in their country. The hope was the insights would enable the auction company to create an innovative offering that would make the export process pain free. Before interviewing a group of exporters about their experiences, we decided we could ask sharper questions if we better understood the end-to-end export process. We called our project "Be the Car."

We watched an exporter purchase a particular car at their auction in Lakeland, Florida. We followed the car from purchase to title check to inspection to transportation on a truck bound for Miami. Once in Miami, the car was placed in a large container, loaded onto a truck, and transported a short distance to customs at the Miami docks. It was inspected and then waited until the right ship arrived. It was then loaded with a large crane onto the ship that set sail for a port in the Black Sea near Zonguldak, Turkey. From there, the car would be loaded onto a train at the Turkish dock and shipped to its ultimate destination.

We talked about the potential for damage at all its many points of loading and unloading. We noticed the many wait times the car had to endure at various stops, especially before being containerized. We were amused that the car had to share a container with a speed boat and two motorcycles. We wondered about the ease of the car getting lost or the likelihood of it missing a connection. When we met with our client to debrief our learnings, he seemed to feel a strong kinship with the car now that we knew so much about its life on its journey by truck, ship, and rail. "What could we learn if we could 'be an exporter'?" It was a sobering moment, as we all realized how deeply we empathized with a car—an inanimate object—yet knew so little about the exporter who owned it until it reached its destination.

How can you "be a customer"?

One of the most revealing questions you can ask a customer is "Tell me about your typical day." Taking an empathy walk (or ridealong or sitalong) involves following a customer through an experience, constantly asking, "What are you experiencing; what are you feeling?" Being a customer is more of an "identification walk." It involves requesting that the customer guide you through an experience he or she would typically have, narrating it along the way. It lets you feel what the customer feels; it is an experience, not a report. And it can be as revealing as phoning your own unit, disguising your voice, and asking for something out of the ordinary.

Seek Second to Understand

Stephen Covey drew from classic books on human relationships to phrase his success habit—"Seek first to understand, then to be understood."[1] And there is more to the habit than simply deferring to another person to go first. The concept is about the pursuit of insight through the demonstration of understanding laced with compassion. The goal of curiosity is to care deeply enough to discover meaning not found merely in the words used. Sometimes creating collective guideposts can help. Again, start first with empathy, then seek to understand.

One approach to this joint search for meaning is to start with a collaborative mindset—that is, a meeting of the minds. "Mindset" is the term for the tone-setting actions at the beginning of a discussion that ensure congruence on three simple but powerful questions. These three questions serve as bannisters to the quality of the conversation. The goal is for both parties to periodically interrupt a long conversation by revisiting the same three questions from my book *Dance Lessons: Six Steps to Great Partnership in Business and Life*.

1. **Why are we here?** Both parties need to be clear on the purpose of the conversation. A simple statement followed by confirmation is usually sufficient: "John, I see this session as an opportunity for the two of us to discuss a new approach for reducing and managing your wait time. Is that your goal as well?"

2. **What will it mean to you/to me?** The potential for both participants to benefit from the dialogue is important. Not only does it help focus the exchange, but it enhances motivation. Proper attention to the potential benefits can turn a lethargic "Here we go again, another meeting with Sandra" mindset into a "Wow, this meeting with Sandra is going to be helpful!" mindset.

3. **How shall we talk?** Mindset also includes telegraphing the tone and style needed. Even if the tone is implied, a brief reminder can be useful in serving notice that an open, candid, freewheeling conversation is needed and expected. It also helps clarify the rules of engagement, avoiding unpleasant surprises: "Edward, I'll be as open and candid as I can in this discussion. My thought was that we devote about thirty minutes to exploring options . . ."[2]

Turn Meaning into Insight

Build-A-Bear Workshop is one example many people think of when considering the idea of customers directly involved in creating a product, service, or solution from which they will benefit. Maxine Clark founded the company in 1997 and was its CEO for sixteen years. There are over four hundred stores today. The concept of "the most fun you'll ever make" has their customers (children) going through an interactive process in which the stuffed animal of their choice is assembled and tailored to their unique preferences during their store visit. It is literally a workshop.

But the backstory is told by Maxine in an interview for *Fortune* in 2012 and puts someone else at the center of her innovative idea. "One day, I was shopping with Katie Burkhardt, the daughter of one of my good friends, and her brother Jack, who collected Ty Beanie Babies. When we couldn't find anything new, Katie picked up a Beanie Baby and said we could make one. She meant we could go home and make the small bears, but I heard something different. Her words gave me the idea to create a company that would allow people to create their own customized stuffed animals." And the rest is history!

Build-A-Bear continues to follow a partnership model that recognizes that the imagination of their customers (like Katie) is their greatest resource. Maxine continues: "There were no formal focus groups, but from the beginning, Build-a-Bear Workshop has had a Cub Advisory Board, which is a group of children who offer their opinions about our products and services. Kids have insights and offer inspiration by looking at the world differently."[3]

The search for meaning is simply the first stop on the path to insight. That is the instant understanding ratchets up to a eureka moment. How do you get to insight? There will be many techniques in the pages ahead, but here are a few quick starter ideas:

- Use an analogy to apply to the customer challenge. If the customer issue were an animal, a sport, a vehicle, etc., what would be its characteristics?

- Choose a role model company for a new lens. If this problem were managed by Starbucks, Amazon, Ritz-Carlton, etc., how would they address it?
- Examine the customer need through one of the five senses. What does the need taste like, smell like, etc.?

Rimini Street is a global provider of enterprise software products and services and the leading third-party support provider for Oracle and SAP software products. Their client base is quite diverse, but all need advanced technical support for their complex environments. Prior to working with them, I did a series of interviews with many of their support professionals. Jennifer Perry, VP of Global SAP Service Delivery, made a profound statement. "When partnering with our clients, they know we are there for them 24/7, provide solutions to their technical issues and are fully invested in their success. Our engineers work extremely hard to provide Rimini Street clients with the best solutions and customer service and seeing this in practice is magical. There are instances where our clients figure it out on their own, sometimes even discover different solutions while working with our engineers, but most every time they end up viewing us as the heroes that helped them win."

Practice Eccentric Listening: The Partnering Crib Notes

Listen without an ulterior motive. Make certain you are listening only to learn, not waiting to make a point or seeking a way to convince, teach, correct, or "sound smart." Listen with your whole body. If you are uncomfortable being silent, deal with it; "listen" and "silent" have the same letters. Look at your customer in a way that would be convincing you are only listening to her or him. Stop "cutting to the chase"; hear all of your customer's story. No multitasking while listening. Don't be a sentence grabber. Be absorbed in what your customer is saying; be inspired by what your customer is meaning. Your ultimate goal is not just collecting information or gaining understanding; your objective is to make your customer feel valued and important. "Listening," wrote actor Alan Alda, "is being able to be changed by the other person."

Conventional wisdom regarding customer relationships suggests, "start with the customer's need." But co-creation partnering is unconventional. It begins with the customer. The need is like a destination; the customer is like the pilot of the transportation. Get to know the pilot, and she or he will take you to where you need to go. Besides, only the pilot knows the shortcuts and the scenic routes.

Listening builds rapport and trust. Unless you build that trust with listening, not much else is going to happen.

—JOHN SAVAGE

CHAPTER 2

Witness Your Customer through an Anthropologist's Lens

You can observe a lot by just watching.

—YOGI BERRA

Because of Winn-Dixie was a 2005 hit movie based on the best-selling novel by Kate DiCamillo. In one scene the movie's star, ten-year-old Opal (played by AnnaSophia Robb), and her new dog Winn-Dixie visit the local storytelling librarian, Miss Franny.

The storyteller spins a tale about her great-grandfather, who created a candy factory that baked feelings of sadness into a sweet candy he called Litmus Lozenges. Miss Franny gave Opal a decorative can of the antique candies to share with her friends. When Opal gave a piece to her seven-year-old best friend, Sweetie Pie, she put the candy in her mouth and exclaimed, "It tastes like not having a dog."[1]

Sweetie Pie's powerful and poignant line got me thinking about how innovation comes from understanding the target dilemma in new ways. When my granddaughter, Annabeth, asked me if rocks could feel, I had to think awhile about her question before giving her an answer that would not risk dispelling her curiosity or dampening her wonderment. Innovation begins with a need or dilemma.

I selected anthropology as the metaphoric customer-understanding lens for a deliberate reason. Psychologists practice their craft to heal, but anthropologists seek only to understand and find insight. Social anthropologists seek to comprehend how people live together in cultures and societies. And they examine without colored lenses or biased ears. Renowned anthropologist Margaret Mead wrote, "Anthropology demands the open-mindedness with which one must look and listen, record in astonishment and wonder that which one would not have been able to guess." It means understanding the customer in new ways to gain new shades of perception.

Wear Your Customer's Moccasins

My wife's hairdresser, Johnny Adair, has been known to get a permanent. When I asked him for his reason for this unique practice, he said, "I see my customers' facial expressions of vulnerability, embarrassment, or discomfort; I want to know more about what I can do to lighten their emotional and physical burden. Experiencing what they go through has enhanced my attention to the details I can manage to make getting a permanent a little less unpleasant."

This is more than simply paying attention to your customer's world to learn what is being experienced and how it can be improved. Like an anthropologist immersing him- or herself in the habits and mores of the people of a culture, Johnny embeds himself rather than simply observing. He is in the performance onstage, not just a spectator in the stands. Curiosity in action is absorption, not just inspection. Such absorption can also come from learning from people who know the customer in special ways. Enter John Longstreet.

When John Longstreet (now CEO of the Pennsylvania Hotel and Restaurant Association) was the general manager of the Harvey Hotel in Plano, Texas, he occasionally served a free breakfast to the taxi drivers who transported guests from his hotel property mostly to DFW airport after their hotel stay. During breakfast he held a focus group discussion to learn more about what drivers learned from his guests. He learned far more than facts; he gained insights, those aha's not likely gleaned from a survey or answers to a "How was your stay?" query from a front desk clerk.

Guests told taxi drivers that hotel bathroom towels with a slight scorched smell were to them not about a careless housekeeper who left them in the dryer too long, but about the potential of a hotel fire. A burned-out security light in the parking lot really meant a perceived lack of security in hotel hallways. Dust balls under the bed signaled bugs on the way. The examination of meaning, not facts, led to a set of insights that created depth to the solutions. When employees gained insights behind common hiccups, their attention to detail and preventive maintenance went up.

Ask, What Would Margaret Mead Do?

Margaret Mead was a renowned cultural anthropologist in the 1960s and '70s and the author of over fifteen books, many breakthroughs in her field. In 1979, Dr. Mead was posthumously awarded the Presidential Medal of Freedom by President Jimmy Carter. When then UN ambassador Andrew Young made the presentation to Mead's daughter, he said, "She mastered her discipline, but she also transcended it. Intrepid, independent, plain spoken, fearless, she remains a model for the young and a teacher from whom all may learn."[2]

Anthropologists study the target of their examination using "frameworks of seeing." These include time, values, traditions, and language. What is the person's or culture's practice of time, what values shape their beliefs, what traditions govern their behavior, and what special words matter or malign? This anthropology mosaic can provide a path to an enriched understanding of your customers in the quest to know them more deeply as well as bolster their trust more fully.

We all have the same amount of *time*, so "out of time" or "late" can signal a low priority. Walmart founder Sam Walton called Procter & Gamble CEO John Smale and announced, "We were going to name you our Supplier of the Year." At the time, P&G was doing over $2 billion worth of business with Walmart. "Were?" asked Smale. Walton continued, "You never returned my call when I called to tell you that. So, we had to name someone else." It triggered a significant shift in how P&G treated Walmart as a customer.[3] Find out what the concept of time means to your customers and manage how the relationships might be threatened with disappointments around time.

All customers have a set of core *values*. Experiences that are in conflict with their values can subconsciously erode their loyalty. Knowing those values enables you to avoid encounters that are dissonant or in conflict. Applying a "values dissonance" lens, a large hotel chain learned that guests' disdain resulted after their affinity program changed control over upgrades from the front desk to the computer. Many guests enjoyed the perception that the friendly person at check-in was making the call on whether they were upgraded to the concierge level. Key learning? Make certain you know the true meaning of your customers' values. Just guessing or assuming "they are just like me" can lead you astray.

Traditions are the customs, mores, and habits shared in a relationship, group, or society. When a customer was invited to a brainstorming meeting, the meeting leader sat at the head of the conference table—a common practice at most organizations. Someone noticed the customer was initially uncomfortable, and politely probed to learn more. The next time the company invited the customer for a discussion, the first question asked was "Where would you prefer to sit?" It was a minor adjustment, but the company reports it was worth the effort since it made them more aware of other traditions that might be practiced by their customers. A conflict of traditions surfaces when your practice fails to jibe with the customer's expectations.

Language means more than communicating in French or Spanish. It means paying attention to the buzzwords, acronyms, and secret lingo reserved for insiders only. A common language (in its broadest sense) can bond and connect; code talking excludes and snubs. When former Alfa Romeo CEO Luca de Meo came from Audi to head up marketing at Volkswagen AG, he realized their global marketing function was filled with gossip. A silo mentality, fueled by an assembly-line linear approach of design to delivery, prevented the cross-pollination of ideas. Without a culture laced with shared meaning, a path to innovation was unlikely. According to authors Linda Hill, Greg Brandeau, Emily Truelove, and Kent Lineback in their book *Collective Genius*, Italian-born Luca learned to speak German so he could converse with his associates directly and not through a translator![4]

Watch Your Customers in Action

Continuum, a Massachusetts-based consulting firm, was hired by Moen Inc. to conduct customer research for use in the development of a new line of showerheads. Continuum felt the best way to really understand what customers wanted in a new showerhead wasn't to ask them via surveys but rather to *watch* them in action. According to the *New York Times*, the company got permission to film customers taking showers in their own homes (I just report this stuff) and used the findings in the new design. Among the insights gleaned were that people spent half their time in the shower with their eyes closed and 30 percent of their time avoiding water altogether. The insights contributed to the new Moen Revolution showerhead becoming a best seller.[5]

We sometimes can't see for looking, can't hear for eavesdropping, and can't appreciate for thinking.
Be with customers as they are, not as you want them to be.

A major hotel chain offered frequent guests a discount on their room rate if they allowed a hotel staff member to follow them to their room to observe their process of unpacking and settling into the guest room. The hotel learned about guest workarounds—small issues never large enough to make the guest comment card. Couples checking in had only one luggage rack to use; guests using their own hairdryer had to unplug the one provided in the bathroom—all small incidents, but when added together with others, they created a negative experience so subtle guests would never mention them.

Never assume you know what customers value. I once stayed at a chain hotel in Philadelphia that did not slide my receipt under my hotel room door the morning I checked out. I was in the lobby at 5 a.m. to catch the first shuttle to the airport for an early morning flight. "Why was my receipt not under my door?" I asked the way-too-perky front desk clerk. His answer: "We want you to come by our front desk to get your receipt so we can bid you a proper farewell." My response: "I think if you asked your guests, they will tell you that the last thing they want at five in the morning, rushing to catch the hotel shuttle bus, is a proper farewell!"

The fun-loving Frisbee wasn't always a toy. Customers changed its character completely. William Frisbie purchased a bakery in the late nineteenth century in Connecticut that he called the Frisbie Pie Company. After his death, his company grew, reaching a peak production of eighty thousand pies per day. One unique feature of the pies was they came packaged in plate-shaped tins embossed with "Frisbie's Pies." But that is the point where the customer took over and created an entirely new product. Yale students discovered they could turn the tins into toys to toss around campus. When the flying disk approached its intended target, the person throwing it shouted "Frisbie" as a warning, much like sounding "fore" on a golf course. Walter Morrison patented the plastic version and sold it to Wham-O.[6] The rest is history. Again, never assume you know what your customers value or that their preferences will remain static.

Learn from the People Who Know

When Cameron Smyth was the mayor of Santa Clarita, north of Los Angeles, he was eager to know what mattered most to his citizens and to gain an appreciation for the issues about which they complained. He knew sending out a survey might not yield the insights needed. He held the city's first annual hairdressers' banquet to learn the real truth. Not only did their gossip turn into the intelligence he sought, he was able to position hairdressers as valuable advocates for the city. The security guard's assessment of the demeanor of a departing key customer can sometimes be more instructive than forty focus groups. Most taxi and limo drivers have X-ray vision. A Google search regarding your customer, including reviews and social media chatter, may give you intelligence a conversation might miss.

Witness Your Customer through an Anthropologist's Lens: The Partnering Crib Notes

Watch the details of your customer being your customer. Take a mental empathy walk tracing your customer's steps through their entire experience with you and your organization. The concept today of customer journey mapping is one my business partner and coauthor, the late Ron Zemke, and I invented in the late 1980s to meticulously understand the customer's world through their eyes. However, we learned that without the customer's affirmation of the map, we could easily miss or misinterpret a customer moment of truth. Be a customer sleuth and look for clues to better understand their world. Examine word choices loaded with insight (like Sweetie Pie's description). Pay attention to the meaning behind what customers communicate. Become a customer whisperer through unprejudiced interpreting. Get intelligence from the customer; get intelligence from people who know the customer.

The skill an anthropologist brings to exploration is partly their astute attention to detail and keen observation acumen. But what separates a great anthropologist from an "also ran" is the ability to remove bias and predisposition from a point of view. They observe and learn like a mirror. Except for the one owned by the evil queen in *Snow White*, a mirror has no opinion on who is the fairest of them all. The objective is to learn deeply about your customers and their proclivities. In a judgment-free arena, there is an evident invitation to surface imaginative ideas, perspectives, and insights.

Innovation starts by intimately observing your customer.

—JEREMY GUTSCHE

CHAPTER 3

Make Customer Inquiry Unleashed and Unfiltered

It is not the answer that enlightens, but the questions.

—EUGÈNE IONESCO

If you want to make granddaughters squeal with delight, take them gold mining. There is an old gold mine a few miles from my river house in North Georgia. Duke's Creek was the site of the first gold discovered in America, by Hernando de Soto in 1540. In 1828, Frank Logan found gold in that same creek and launched America's first gold rush. The dirt purchased in buckets for granddaughters to pan comes from that same gold mine nearby. And the result can make a granddaughter a rock star at school on "show and tell" day.

Panning for gold is a lot like searching for insight. It is not always easy. Panning for gold works like this. First, you put a double handful of sand in a shallow heavy-gauge steel pan and dip the pan in the water, filling it half full. Second, you must have a strong faith there is gold in the bottom of this mixture, enabling you to be patient during its extraction. Next, you gently move the pan back and forth as small amounts of yellow sand wash over the side of the pan.

The objective is to let the black sand sink to the bottom of the pan. But this is the point where panning for gold gets really serious. Impatience or strong-arming the way the pan is shaken means the black sand escapes over the side along with the yellow sand. Once black sand is the only sand left in the pan, you are rewarded with flecks of gold. The gold resides among the black sand since both are heavier than the yellow sand.

The pursuit of insight can be like panning for gold in the sand. Insight is generally not lying on top, ready to be found and polished. If it were easy pickings, it would have already been found. Insight lies beneath the obvious and ordinary. It is lodged in the dark sands of irrational beliefs, myths, fears, prejudices, and biases. It lurks under untested hunches, ill-prepared starts, and unfortunate mistakes. Extracting insight takes patience and persistence. It cannot be rushed and haphazardly forced. And, most of all, it cannot be strong-armed; it must be discovered.

Show Your Earnest, Curious Intent

The ritual happens thousands of times every day in restaurants around the country. You are in the middle of your meal, and the maître d' or manager approaches your table with the query "How is everything?" And you politely respond, "Fine," unless something is really, really bad or really, really good. The inquirer thinks an evaluation has been rendered by the customer; the customer believes a fair-weather, friendly greeting has been delivered.

The question is only a question in its form, not its intent. Sure, it has a question mark at the end, but that is just for show. Think of it like the greeting you use most mornings when you arrive at work: "Good morning, how are you doing?" You are not expecting the respondent to give you the lowdown on how his kid is flunking out of third grade, or how she is behind on a mortgage payment, or the fact that he has a dull ache in his lower back. Frankly, you were just saying hello.

So go ahead and let your opening inquiry be a friendly greeting. The real test of the intent of the inquirer is the second question—the question after the question. It signals the true intent of the dialogue—am I sincerely curious, with a desire to learn, or am I here simply to be friendly? The intent is always the challenge of genuine inquiry. And inquiry, the deliberate search for meaning from another, is one of the three applications of curiosity-driven innovation.

The complexity of unleashed and unfiltered inquiry requires far more than just using a set of communication tactics guaranteed to enrich a conversation. It is an entire personal repertoire of attitudes, actions, and adventures aimed at unlocking the secrets behind the customer's mask. Your customer is the sentinel of wisdom at the door on the other side of his or her eyes. Whether you get in the door or get to plunder in secret closets of wisdom depends on the rapport you establish, the authenticity you model, and the openness you boldly demonstrate.

Stew Leonard's farm-fresh food store is a pioneer in the grocery store category. Started by Stew Sr. in 1969, the company now has seven stores in Connecticut, New York, and New Jersey and is famous for their singular focus on their customers. Not only is Stew Leonard's in *The Guinness Book of World Records* for having the highest retail sales per square foot of any grocery store in the world, it was on *Fortune*'s "100 Best Companies to Work For" list for ten consecutive years. The company leadership regularly leads a focus group with customers. Not only do they get helpful feedback, they have historically gotten great innovation, in some cases customer-originated breakthroughs.

"Why don't you put your strawberries out in a big pile straight from the farmer instead of putting them in little quart baskets?" a customer suggested in such a focus group years ago. Now that practice is standard in the industry. And their strawberry sales tripled. "Why don't you let us buy fresh fish right off the ice straight from the Boston harbors instead of packaging them?" Stew set up a fish bar like a fish market, something new in the grocery industry at that time. Their packaged fish sales did not decrease, and they doubled their fish sales overall. "The reason they tell us," Stew Sr. says, "is that we react."[1]

Query with Unleashed Boldness and Unfiltered Freedom

Unleashed inquiry is the gallant step forward to ask that odd, out-of-left-field question without reservation or reticence. Assume that someone before you already interviewed your customer and asked all the predictable questions. He or she did not learn anything that was not already known or was surprising. It is now your job to craft questions that will take your customer in new, fresh directions. Here is an example.

A bank in Nicaragua wanted to learn more about their customers so they could create new tailored solutions. They had been using the Net Promoter survey crafted around the question "Would you recommend our bank to a family member or friend?" The bank survey manager was encouraged to also ask customers, "Have you recommended our bank?" Customer surveys were anonymous, but customers were given an opportunity to include their name and contact information, and many did. One bank employee suggested the bank conduct focus groups with some of the identifiable customers who indicated they had recommended the bank. The pay dirt question asked in the focus group was "What can we do to make it easier for you to recommend us?" The answer: give me a bank employee's business card I can pass to a friend or family member. It turned out to be a major success.

Partnership inquiry should never be locked and loaded—locked on assumptions or loaded with biases.

Unfiltered means letting go, completely relinquishing any effort to control or manipulate the outcome. It is an effort to yield pure, raw truth (or at least the customer's undiplomatic perception of the truth). It includes putting all effort into being completely authentic, real, and mask free. Letting go involves being devoted to learning, not dedicated to convincing or guarding.

Unfiltered curiosity is all about genuineness. There is a cleanness about relationships in which authenticity is valued. It means being caring enough to be honest, curious and learning-oriented enough to invite and accept candor. It starts with a countenance of curiosity. Next, it entails being excited about dissonant data—think of it as the black sand that alerts you that you are getting closer to the gold. Remember, when customers offer a negative critique, it is a test of your sincerity regarding whether you can "handle the truth." If you put your energy into defending, explaining, or rationalizing, they will shut the door on your getting any more authentic information.

Use Open-Ended, Interesting Questions

The conventional wisdom on questioning has always been to ask open-ended questions. Closed questions, the lesson goes, will cause the receiver to deliver a single-word or short-phrase answer. However, the process is more complicated than that. Anyone with a teenager knows that the answers to questions beginning with "what," "how," and "why" can yield answers as short as those for a yes-no question.

A large dental-practice company held ideation sessions on creating standards for their many offices on how best to serve children who came to their offices for dental maintenance or procedures. This was a faith-based company with the mission statement "Serve God in all that we do." They had invited a group of parents to help generate ideas. Not surprisingly, the question "What would Jesus do?" came up rather early. But the breakthroughs came when a parent asked, "Jesus? What would Mickey do?" It led to "What if Dora designed your smocks? What if Barbie selected the music?"

The goal of insight-seeking questioning is not just more words in the answer, but more depth in the thinking needed to produce the answer. Craft interesting questions that make customers reflect before they report. "What is one thing that makes your experience memorable?" might be more exciting than "What do you like most about our restaurant?" Rather than asking, "What can we do better?" you might try, "If you owned this retail store and wanted your customers to have an awesome experience, what would you do?"

Albert Einstein wisely said, "It's not that I'm so smart, but I stay with the questions much longer." Staying with questions longer enables you to demonstrate curiosity. Sincere curiosity tells customers you genuinely care about them and their point of view. The byproduct is not just more information or greater understanding. It is the insight that becomes the roadmap on your path to an innovative solution for customers.

Dream a Little Dream with Customers

Jeff Immelt, when CEO of General Electric, held Dreaming Sessions with key customers. The goal was to think, together, about where their goals and relationships would be in five to ten years. When John Byrne of *Fast Company* magazine asked Jeff to describe such a session, Immelt described it this way: "We had the railroad CEOs in with their operating people. We spent half a day, grounding ourselves on where the industry is, where we are, what their trends are, and then said, 'Okay, here are some things to think about: higher fuel, more West-East shipments because of imports from China.' We would have four or five boundary conditions. And then we'll ask, 'If you had $200 million to $400 million to spend on R&D at GE, how would you prioritize it?'"[2] You may not have $400 million to spark your customers' dreams, but finding ways for them to give voice to their hopes and aspirations will enrich your inquiry into your customers' imagination.

Never forget your customers' needs are nomadic. My wife recently bought a brand-new Lexus SUV. It came with a navigation system built into the dash. I think it looks really slick! It will alert you when there is a traffic accident many miles ahead and tell you how long the upcoming traffic delay will last, with alternative routes around the delay. It monitors all the systems of your vehicle and sends you an alert if there is anything out of the ordinary. You get a reminder if your tires need air, your oil needs changing, or your shoelace is untied. I was just kidding about the shoe part . . . but you get the point!

A week after she bought the car with the cool navigation system in the dash, she put her old Garmin GPS on top of the dash and plugged it into the cigarette lighter! It was her test. Sure enough, her Garmin was showing roads not known by the navigation system. When the GPS on the dash and the navigation system in the dash differed on the "best route," the GPS always gave the best, most up-to-date advice.

"It's the satellite," she explained. "The navigation system is information programmed into a CD months ago. It stays the same until you go to the dealership and update it. But the GPS stays updated . . . real time."

Customer needs are a lot like the landscape. They change all the time, not just annually when you are about to send out the big survey. Smart providers figure out ways to build customer GPSs into every customer touch point. When a customer has a hiccup in Des Moines, the distribution center in San Jose knows about it. When a quorum of disgruntled customers registers a complaint on social media, a strike team is triggered to search for root causes and implement an appropriate fix. Get rid of your old customer navigation system and put your customer GPS on your dash.

Make Customer Inquiry Unleashed and Unfiltered: The Partnering Crib Notes

Talk with your customer like an old friend, not at them. Start with questions your customer will enjoy answering. Make a habit of being jarringly candid and completely genuine. Forget about your in-charge-role persona; use your best friend persona. Help your customer have a meaningful conversation by not quality-controlling every misstatement (if you are clear on the meaning). Great conversations fueled by unfiltered inquiry flow easily; they are not jerky or halting. Remember, a great conversation with a customer is not debate practice. Be a learner, not an interrogator. Speak your customer's language. Ask more questions than you need to ask in order to know the answer. Use warm eye hugs (you get it!), not glaring or intimidating stares. Start with safe dreamer questions—"What would it be like in the future if . . ." This is a quest of insight in a crucible of imagination. Make your inquiry feel free and fun to your customers.

A Look Ahead: Grounding

"Give me a place to stand, and a lever long enough, and I will move the world," wrote Archimedes. It was his famous description of the principle of leverage. But it is also a key principle of co-creation. The lever is the customer's imagination, and it can move a customer's need and aspiration to an innovative result. But like the principle of leverage, the partnership requires a place to stand. In the next secret, we will explore the power of purpose as that place and purpose's role in generating collective focus, shaping value-based relationship governors, and championing an "I am the warranty" outlook that ensures co-creation partnerships are successful.

Doubt comes in at the window when
inquiry is denied at the door.

—BENJAMIN JOWETT

Secret 2

GROUNDING

Partner on Purpose

Definiteness of purpose is the starting point of all achievement.

—W. CLEMENT STONE

I was staying at a hotel in Richmond and arrived very early for their breakfast buffet, before it was completely arranged. The employee in charge of setup picked up on my happy-go-lucky, "take your time" attitude and took a risk. "Are you a get-involved kinda guy or are you more of a wait and watch type?" I indicated I was the former.

"Okay, would you like some early morning amusement?" she asked with an impish tone. "You bet!" I replied. "Then grab that cereal dispenser and waffle maker over there and set 'em up next to the juice machines like this was gonna be an awesome breakfast party." Within a few minutes the buffet was ready. I felt as if I owned the place. But wait, there's more.

As I was enjoying my first cup of coffee while waiting for a colleague to join me to go through the buffet line, the hotel employee sat down at my table. "I see you in here every few months. What do you do?" I explained I was a customer loyalty consultant and ran a training program for a Richmond client headquartered nearby. "Amazing," she said, seeming genuinely impressed. "I don't get a guest service expert in here very often, at least that I am aware of. How would you describe our breakfast buffet?"

"It is plain vanilla," I said, sensing she was looking for direct candor, not an easy compliment. "I completely agree," she said, "and our mission is to pursue memorable excellence. So, what would you do to make this buffet better?" She pulled her chair up closer.

"Kumquats," I said. "Why do you say that?" she asked, sensing my answer was more metaphor than a specific recommendation. I continued, "What can you do that would make the breakfast experience unique and unusual, with something people would mention at work after their meal here? The usual fare might be fine, but if it is not memorable, there is less of a reason for customers to come back, other than sheer convenience."

My next trip to the hotel two months later had a pleasant surprise. In addition to the usual strawberries, honeydew, and cantaloupe on the buffet line, there was mango and papaya. And here is the best part. Right beside the juice bar was a whimsical container full of little bright-colored umbrellas you could add to your juice glass. Now I not only felt as if I owned the place, I felt as if I helped create it. When the meeting planner mentioned that the company was looking at a different hotel for their training program, I quarreled like a kid having to give up a favorite toy.

GROUNDING

Together We Preserve Focus

The pursuit of innovation with customers starts with the "why." It is the raison d'être that lends meaning to focus and relevance to the union. The relationship must have a grounding focus—a collaborative quest to solve a customer problem or improve or create a service or product your customer values. In our hotel example, the hotel buffet person had a mission—"pursue memorable excellence." She knew memorable excellence was in the eyes of her guests. She created an interpersonal welcome mat for my imagination to be applied to her hotel brand and my hotel loyalty. And she took even further what we had discovered together on our imagination path by adding tiny, colorful umbrellas.

The innovation quest also requires intentional toil and focused energy. Again, the subtitle of this secret has a double meaning, on *purpose*—meaning grounded in a mission, vision, or purpose—and *on* purpose—meaning deliberate, intentional, and planned. One interpretation suggests a solid foundation with roots in a customer hope and aspiration. The other interpretation means a serious and thoughtful commitment to making something happen that has meaning.

Let's recap. The imagination of your customer is something he or she owns and defends. Under the right circumstances, your customer is willing to share this special treasure. Again, your customer also has an itch that needs to be scratched, so to speak, and needs your help in scratching it. "Scratching itches" is merely a metaphor for meeting a customer's need and/or solving a customer's problem in a novel way. Scratching itches requires the blending of your imagination with theirs.

You gain access to your customer's imagination in two ways: by invitation or by attraction. Invitation is a welcome, a polite urging through your interpersonal manners—the listening, understanding, and inquiring covered in Secret 1. Attraction, on the other hand, is an alluring call or stimulating interest. You are *invited* to a party; you are *attracted* to a circus. In the pages ahead, we will unearth how grounding performs this attracting function. Grounding (whether it is labeled mission, vision, goal, or focus) is present in every innovation culture. Productive innovation is not chaotic creativity; it is purposeful imagination in action.

Some may suggest a customer-provider relationship start with purpose or grounding—beginning with the end in mind. However, the focus, vision, or mission becomes clearer if the partnership is first crafted and fortified through curiosity. Love at first sight might have triggered your private vision of a long-term personal relationship ("Someday I am going to marry this person"), but you likely did not pop the nuptial question on your first date.

Grounding has three parts. A focus (or target) on which the energies of the partnership are directed, guardrails that help keep the union on course in an effective manner, and a warranty that bolsters full accountability for ensuring the relationship achieves its goal (figure 4).

FIGURE 4. Components of grounding

Grounding represents the core need or aspiration of your customer. If that core need is clearly defined, deeply sourced, and purely presented, it can be as attractive as an adventure, as enchanting as an artistic or athletic display, and as compelling as a contest. The collective process of defining, clarifying, and staging an imagination adventure helps bond and benefit all involved as well as all impacted. While curiosity greases the skids of enticement so your customer's imagination is exported, grounding draws your customer's imagination through its irresistible pull. Think of grounding as having a magnetic force rather than a purely invitational one.

Grounding is the basic foundation for an innovative outcome. As such, it functions as the groundwater of purpose and thus the source of psychic energy for the innovation process. However, there must be guardrails to help the partnership retain focus, while informing the relationship's "rules of engagement." Even the most familiar creativity tool on the planet—brainstorming—has guidelines that help make it effective.

The purposeful (full of purpose) components of grounding require a meeting of the minds on a shared focus. But if you are to work with customers to attract the gifts of their imagination, you need more than simply a target. There must be some interpersonal boundaries to your working togetherness. Rules are typically the antithesis of the freedom-loving innovation process; guardrails are needed to ensure there are clear boundaries and agreements on the interpersonal etiquette that ensures effective collaboration. Done well, all parties view themselves as the architects of their union and the inventors of its results.

Guardrails need a loose-tight feature that provides discipline without being an unwelcome governor on imagination and inventiveness. They provide relationship protocols as well as value-based fences to keep the alliance out of weeds and rabbit holes.

Grounding also means all parties assume the full warranty for the health and longevity of the partnership. Co-creation partnerships that prosper reject selfishness; they are all about "How can I serve you?" What sidetracks too many provider-customer relationships is the one-sidedness of one party's personal investment in the partnership's sustainability. But when all parties assume full and complete responsibility for making their relationship work, it will always succeed. This "the-buck-stops-with-me" assertion mandates a steadfast commitment to the process of partnering. It is this feature that cultivates resilience, robustness, and tenacity.

Grounding is the sentinel of relationship security. It acts as a shepherd—out front running interference on all things that could threaten the coalition. More than simply protection, the goal of grounding is to retain clarity of focus, maintain mutual commitment to results, and foster undivided attention (as in resisting distraction). If the co-creation partnership were a vehicle of ingenuity, grounding would be the dashboard in front of its drivers.

CHAPTER 4

Put Insight in Focus

The only way of discovering the limits of the possible is to venture a little way past them in the impossible.

—ARTHUR C. CLARKE

There is a beautiful golf course at the beginning of my long driveway. My lakefront home backs up to the shoreline but fronts the thirteenth tee box. A Jack Nicklaus-designed PGA course, it is the setting for many golf tournaments. While the thirteenth hole is breathtaking—you play 434 yards straight into the lake—it is the fourteenth hole that gets the golfers' laments in the bar at the end of an arduous eighteen holes.

Almost the entire fourteenth hole is played over the water where the lake shoreline cuts deep into the golf course. Despite the fact that it is a mere 186-yard par-three hole, many a golfer has been psychologically distracted by the giant water trap and had their golf balls land in the water. But the best golfers know a secret—focus only on the hole and don't get distracted by the fact that your golf ball will be flying over water.

It is a mighty lesson for co-creation partnerships. Insight in focus means the creation of a captivating target at which to aim. But it is more than simply a line of sight for creative energy. It is viewing the target as an emotional pull, thus the added adjective, captivating. That means letting the target serve as a magnetic attraction, not just as a directional intent. Attraction is the reason great missions and visions are often referred to as "a calling"—they summon you to duty rather than just expecting your commitment. Like a Pied Piper of purpose, they compel you to join in.

When I was in infantry officer candidate school at Fort Benning, Georgia, a part of the training was learning to become a sharpshooter with a rifle. A sharpshooter designation is the highest level of marksmanship a soldier could attain; the sharpshooter badge qualified me for sniper school, had I had an interest. My success on the rifle range came from odd advice from the sergeant in charge. "The rifle is not the big player in this activity," he told me. "It is just you and the target; the rifle works for you both. Be so at one with your target that it pulls the bullet from your rifle barrel. Be so focused on precision that it seems as if the rifle fired itself, leaving you surprised." Olympic gold medal shooters say championship shooting is an intuitive process, not a mechanical one.

Mutual focus is essential to co-creation partnering. It means there is such a collective focus on the target that you both are surprised when the creative synapses in your brains are fired and an innovative solution emerges. This chapter will outline a series of techniques designed to help pull the ideas from your imaginations. We begin with the outlook or stance needed for effective focus.

In chapter 3 ("Make Customer Inquiry Unleashed and Unfiltered") we began with a description of panning for gold. A small point in that example was mentioned but not discussed. Here it is again: "Second, you must have a strong faith there is gold in the bottom of this mixture, enabling you to be patient during its extraction." There are several benefits to faith or belief. It will not only support perseverance, it will help animate your search for focus. Faith is like an agreement you make with yourself that, despite temptations and distractions from other factors, you will remain totally true to the course. It is part of the magical force that pulls the bullet toward the target.

A large hospital in Rochester, Minnesota, held a leadership session on initiating a change management plan to become patient centered. As the session opened, the CEO announced to his leadership team and physician's council, "Before we can convince our patients we are a patient-centered hospital, we must be ourselves convinced; not just lip service, but 'I'll-give-at-least-a-day-a-week-to-make-this-happen' type involvement." He reminded them of the difference between the two perspectives by telling the well-worn story of a chicken and a pig viewing a billboard together near their field that proclaimed the upcoming "ham and eggs week." "If you are as committed as the chicken, we are not ready," he told his leaders. "We need to be willing to be involved like the pig to make this work." They elected to wait to start the initiative until they had more "pigs."

Focus requires seeing the collective target in sharp color, with all around it in blurred black and white.

"Without a dream, you cannot have a dream come true," wrote the late best-selling author Zig Ziglar. Your goal is to help your customer's dream come true. But getting the customer's imagination to be drawn to that dream requires nurturing a passion for it. It means taking the customer's need and aspiration beyond a ho-hum task to be done and framing it into a deeper, more profound purpose. Remember the bricklayers' responses to the "What are you men doing" query? Your collective goal is to surface a "cathedral-building" focus rather than a "brick-laying" mindset. And in this important endeavor, a picture is worth a thousand words.

Start with a Picture of Your Customer's Goal

TravelCenters of America (TA) is the largest full-service travel-center company in the United States, serving professional drivers and motorists alike. My friend John DiJulius, author of *The Relationship Economy*, and his company, The DiJulius Group, consulted with them on culture change.[1] Frontline employees daily deal with countless demanding drivers upset their truck needs repair and worried about truck downtime. To change TA's culture required altering employees' mindsets to focus on the "plight of the driver." The DiJulius Group held brainstorming sessions with TA executives, employees, and most importantly, their customers—truck drivers. They needed a picture-making focus for this co-creation effort. The truck drivers helped them better understand the demands of being away from home for long stretches, fluctuations in demand, fear of layoffs, mechanical issues, and family commitments. Some drivers talked about the guilt they felt from being away and missing their children's events.

The result? TravelCenters of America created a training video titled *A Day in the Life of a Driver*. It depicted the typical day of a driver who has not been home for an extended period of time. His goal is to make it home for his son's basketball game that evening. He has not seen his son play all season. He finds out more drivers with whom he works are being laid off, making him concerned for his job. He finally makes all his stops and is headed home to see his son's game when one of his tires blows. You realize he probably is not going to see his son's game. The video shows the driver pulling into a TravelCenters of America truck repair location. The cliff-hanger makes employees eager to say, just like the employee in the video, "I got this one; I got this next driver coming in," with a determination to get him back on the road and home in time. TravelCenters has repositioned their employees' mindset to "How can I be a hero today?"

Surfacing the customer's imagination came through getting truck drivers to characterize their needs and hopes in a very personal manner—the responsibility of being a good parent, the coping with fatigue and distress, and the disappointment of a truck-down situation at a crucial time. It elevated the hope of getting a great customer experience to more than simply fulfilling a basic need. For TravelCenters, learning their customers' deeper hopes surfaced their frontline yearning to be a hero much like a firefighter saving a child from a burning building. The blending of these hopes became the springboard for the innovative solution they created.

Blend Your Pictures into One

Blending is a synergistic process of mixing different visions into one that is greater than the sum of its parts. It requires listening and valuing, not dominating and winning. It is a collaborative (co-laboring) effort in which all features of competition are removed from the exploration. One approach is for provider and customer to draw a picture of their focus on a flip chart, compare charts, and discuss features of each that can expand, enrich, or enhance its meaning and message. Think of it as an ad campaign you are together pitching to a company or prospect. Consider it as a prototype you are preparing for a design team to turn into a rendering, like a sculpture, picture, or performance.

Blended pictures painted the color of purpose attract imagination and captivate conviction. And they can take many forms. For a meeting between a quick-service coffee chain and a group of their customers, the objective was the creation of a drive-thru that would fit in the corner of a shopping center. There were obstacles to overcome and challenges to address. The meeting started by having company leaders and customers work in separate groups with Legos and Matchbox cars, constructing a mock-up of how a drive-thru could work. They compared constructions and explored similarities. By the end, their focus was clear, but most importantly, it was congruent.

Marriott's Meeting Imagined website enables meeting planners to go on a Pinterest-type site, create their unique, differentiated meeting, and then work with the onsite meeting staff to implement their design. Again, clarity and congruence of collective visions are vital.

Create a Clear Focus

So, let's practice with a made-up situation. You are the head of sales for a major hotel. Your primary clients are business groups scheduling meetings at your property. One of your largest clients wants their meetings to be more engaging. The meeting planner schedules a meeting with you and your staff. Here is a framework to organize the focus.

- What is your primary goal or aim? Boil it down to a paragraph. Now down to two sentences.
- If you elevated your two sentences to be at the "ensure world peace and solve world hunger" level of aspiration, how might it sound?
- What is the end memory you would want your customers to talk about with others? What does it sound like? Create a short one-paragraph script.
- If your event were to be nominated for a major award in the future, what would be its top selling points?
- What are the top OMGs (oh my goodnesses) you need to avoid and remember?

Test Your Focus: Are You Addressing the Right Problem?

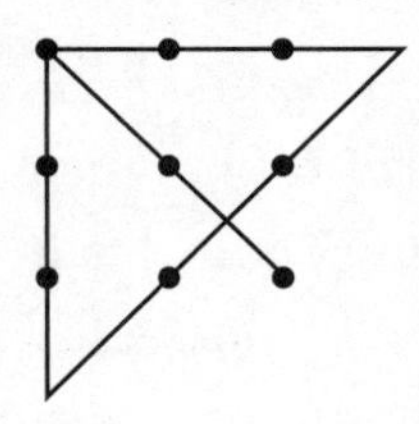

Most adults in the modern world have seen the "connect-the-nine-dots" puzzle (connect all nine dots with four straight lines without lifting the pencil). Its solution requires challenging the made-up, false assumption that you cannot go outside the area of the nine dots. "In challenging assumptions," wrote Edward de Bono in his classic book, *Lateral Thinking*, "one must challenge the necessity of boundaries and limits and the validity of individual concepts."[2] Providers, like all humans, can suffer from "functional fixedness"—the tendency to fixate on the way in which a product or service has always been used, making it hard to see an alternative view.

Kimberly-Clark was told by their customers that they didn't want their toddlers to wear diapers. They also did not want them to wet the bed. It took customers to help Kimberly-Clark break their "functional fixedness" to challenge beliefs and discover the pull-up diaper, not only a breakthrough product, but also a completely new product category.[3]

What beliefs are the foundation of the customer's challenge and your innovation goal? Take time to list them and examine closely. Make certain the beliefs are real, not myth. When I was a teenager and my grandfather heard me resist a chore by questioning whether it was doable, he would test that view by asking, "If I gave you a million dollars and a shotgun, could you get it done?" It was amazing how many times "I can't" turned out to be "I prefer not to." Assumptions and beliefs are innovation blindfolds you sometimes don't know you are wearing until they are cross-examined.

View Your Customer's Need as a Paradigm Shift

Ted Levitt made the point in his book *The Marketing Imagination* that no one ever bought a quarter-inch drill bit because they collected drill bits for display on the living room wall; they sought a quarter-inch hole.[4] Sometimes ideation with customers can lose sight of the hole paradigm and get sidetracked by clinging to a drill-bit paradigm. Be clear about "Why are we here . . . really?" History is filled with companies that did drill-bit thinking. Large movie companies failed to appreciate that the TV explosion in the 1950s needed content, and watched NBC fill that need. Motels along interstate highways in the 1950s were started by upstarts like Holiday Inn instead of giant hotel companies, who were blinded by a "hotels" paradigm instead of an "away-from-home-lodging" paradigm.

Chick-fil-A is arguably the most loved fast-food restaurant in the country. One of its ads sports the tagline "We didn't invent the chicken, just the chicken sandwich." It is the punchline of a partnership backstory that highlights the willingness of Chick-fil-A to think outside the chicken yard. In 1964, a Georgia poultry supplier was hired by an airline to supply them with skinless chicken breasts for the plastic trays of in-flight meals. He ended up with too many chicken breasts that did not comply with the airline's size requirements. He asked Chick-fil-A founder Truett Cathy if he could use them.[5] Cathy could have said, "We sell burgers." Instead, his company became the largest chicken restaurant in the world.

Think outside the usual paradigm in which your customer's need resides. Consider whether this focus is a part of something much larger. Strategic questions can help you ensure your focus is relevant and important. Use the ten questions in the sidebar for that assessment.

TEN QUESTIONS FOR ASSESSING FOCUS, CLARITY, AND RELEVANCE

1. Could this problem or issue be better solved if outsourced?
2. Are you and your customer solving the right problem or issue?
3. If the solution you discovered failed to work, who would be harmed?
4. Who would benefit?

5. Might this be your customer's hobby horse and not the significant challenge your customer is presenting?
6. What would happen if you elected to do nothing, to take a pass?
7. What would be the impact if your organization made this its number one concern?
8. Are you partnering for the right focus?
9. Are you partnering for the right focus but with the wrong partner?
10. What would signal that this problem or issue needed to be automated, eliminated, or exchanged for an alternative?

Put Insight in Focus: The Partnering Crib Notes

The test of an insight focus is to make certain you are addressing the right problem, issue, or challenge. It is always helpful to ask, Is this the problem or just a symptom? Collective root-cause analysis not only helps zero in on the proper focus, it can ramp up enthusiasm for resolution and ensure joint clarity. The quality tool called Five Whys can help melt away distractions, leaving a raw, unadorned target for disciplined focus. Five Whys is patterned after a child continually asking "why" to any answer to his or her question. The goal is to unearth the root cause. If your customer gets defensive about protecting a sacred, long-held view, avoid elevating defensiveness through challenge. Instead, ask questions that help facilitate a new perspective. Does the focus have a jump-start quality that makes your heart race? Is your customer's focus compatible with your organization's vision, values, and capacity?

When Chinese motorcycle maker Loncin wanted to compete effectively against Suzuki, Yamaha, and Honda in the Vietnamese market, their marketing analyses determined their motorcycles were viewed by prospects as too expensive. Established wisdom suggested they talk with customers to find unique ways to add value or perceived value to justify the higher cost. However, rather than turn to customers, Loncin partnered with their suppliers to identify ways to lower manufacturing costs. The hundreds of ideas generated resulted in a 70 percent decrease in costs that translated to a 60 percent increase in market share. Armed with new capabilities, the company expanded into engines and cars.[6]

Goal setting is similar to traveling from point A to point B within a city. If you clearly understand what the goal is, you will definitely reach the destination because you know its address.

—THOMAS ABREU

CHAPTER 5

Construct Value-Based Guardrails

The chief enemy of creativity is "good" sense.

—PABLO PICASSO

Miss Lena Hartley, bless her heart, was wrong. And she really was trying to be helpful. But sure as rain, she was wrong.

When Nancy Marie Rainey of Walnut Ridge, Arkansas, gave a "yes" answer to my "Will you be my life partner?" question, it was one of the happiest days of my life. But getting married in the Deep South in the 1960s was not without challenges. In particular, it meant getting the blessing of the guardians of local civility and protocol—the Women's Missionary Circle #4 of the First Baptist Church in my hometown.

The setting for this important rite was a shower for my bride-to-be sponsored by Circle #4. The fact that I was marrying an assertive, razor-sharp Arkansas girl imposed a special inspection requirement on these well-meaning ladies. Not only was she from out of town, but as far as they were concerned, she may not have really been from the South. Now to a Northerner, this may sound peculiar. Arkansas is not exactly New Jersey, but it isn't Alabama-Mississippi-Georgia-Tennessee either! So, the shower lasted a little longer than normal.

Boys were not invited to showers. The women in the Circle always referred to the opposite gender as "boys," no matter their age. The "boys" sat in their trucks and cars in the church parking lot waiting to drive home their wives, girlfriends, moms, or brides-to-be when the shower finally ended. And of course, shower-waiting had rituals as rich as shower-attending.

Grooms-to-be were allowed by the ladies of Circle #4 to come into the social room only at the very end of the shower to help load up all the loot! There was, however, an expectation that any male intruder give the appropriate "oo's" and "ah's" when cued with a "Come look at this!" It was also the opportunity for one of the senior ladies to pull the groom-to-be aside and render the verdict from their bride-to-be inspection. Having talked with some of the "ol' boys" during the shower-waiting part, I had learned a bit about the ladies' special scoring system.

The highest score you could get was "You don't deserve her," usually pronounced after a stern "Boy!" and a very long pause. That designation, however, was typically reserved for a member of the high school homecoming court whose family's family's family had helped charter the church. "Lovely" and "special" were the next best category. The barely passing grade was usually a collective pronouncement like "I know you two will be very happy." Miss Lena was the chosen pronouncer.

I was passing by the choir rehearsal room on my way to the car with an armful of gifts when she almost timidly pulled me aside. The look on her face telegraphed her dilemma. This inspection was unique. My assertive, high-spirited, obviously very bright bride-to-be from out of town (and possibly out of the South) had defied their grading protocols.

"Be tolerant," she said. I was confused! Was this a grade the ol' boys had missed, a piece of advice, or a roundabout way of admitting, "We don't know how to grade who you have chosen? So . . . go and be tolerant!"? Then she added, "You'll do fine if you're just tolerant." Over the next fifty-plus years, I learned that Miss Lena was "in the right church but the wrong pew."

Give Your Partnership Flexibility, Not Tolerance

McDonald's is famous for its careful faithfulness to its offerings and practices. However, it was not corporate that originated the decision to offer breakfast, it was one of their customers—a franchisee named Herb Peterson. Franchisees are customers to corporate; the burger buyer is more of a consumer to corporate. In 1972, Peterson showed McDonald's chairman Ray Kroc a breakfast sandwich idea he had created and tested. He had a local blacksmith create a ring to keep the egg and yolk contained while being cooked. Kroc loved the idea and asked Peterson for other breakfast ideas. Within twenty years, McDonald's was making $5 billion a year on breakfast alone.

Let's look closely at this customer imagination at play example. First, Herb was a man of imagination. He coined McDonald's first national advertising slogan, "Where quality starts fresh every day." Herb's son described him this way: "When my dad was let loose in a kitchen, he was half creative genius and half mad scientist."

But the real backstory is the willingness of Ray Kroc to "un-governor" the imagination capacity of franchisees (his customers) to contribute to the company's venturing into new creations. McDonald's was the first quick-service restaurant chain to offer breakfast, starting with Peterson's Egg McMuffin. Kroc was famous for his innovation. One of his initial contacts after acquiring the first McDonald's franchise in 1955 was his friend Walt Disney, whom he called about opening a restaurant in what would become Disneyland.[1] But consider what McDonald's would have missed had Kroc rigidly responded to Herb's breakfast sandwich idea with "Herb, you just don't understand your franchise agreement." Assume your customers have similar gifts waiting to be sourced and used.

All successful partnerships require give and flex; they expand to accommodate. Tolerance-based relationships are exercises in sufferance. There is a degree of rigidity about them. Such unyielding relationships have the volume turned up on every flaw and error. People in relationships based on tolerance are perpetually pained by partner imperfections but silently suffer without comment. There is a kind of resignation, as in "This unfortunate disruption just 'comes with the territory.'" When the customer's imagination is in the driver's seat, the last thing needed to encourage a wide-open throttle is a passenger (a.k.a. provider) who is intent on backseat driving.

Thomas Edison's famous assessment of his efforts to create an incandescent light is a classic example of give-and-flex elasticity. "Results! Why, man, I have gotten a lot of results. I know several thousand things that won't work." At the core of his self-acceptance was an attitude of adventure and the assumption of goodness, not a blunder demanding chastisement through guilt, blame, criticism, or rejection. Partnerships with customers that nurture a spirit of innovation work just like that. There is an optimistic, vibrant other-acceptance that fosters a freedom to go forward. It is an interpersonal alliance that clothes hiccups in a coat of many colors, not black and white.

Jeff Toister, author of *Getting Service Right*, sends a newsletter to thousands of customer service professionals. The idea came from a client. Here is Jeff's description of how it all happened.

> *The idea was hatched over a cup of coffee with a client of mine, Sue Thompson. At the time, she ran the transportation and parking department at Oregon Health and Science University. Thompson had hired me to facilitate customer service training for her team and they had since done a remarkable job creating a positive reputation on campus. Now, she was concerned about sustaining the momentum. Thompson regularly discussed service with her employees, but she wanted to add an outside perspective.*
>
> *We put our heads together and sketched out a solution right there in the coffee shop. I created a series of weekly reminders to email to Thompson's team. Each week, her employees received a simple email with one tip based on what was covered in training. The reminders worked so well I quickly decided to make them available for free to anyone who wanted to sign up to my website.*[2]

Construct Value-Based Guardrails

Consider this scenario. You are the managing partner of a medical clinic. Several years ago, you created a board of patients comprising ten patients who meet monthly with you and your physician's leadership group. The patients want to focus this month on how to reduce patient wait. It is a joint issue since there are actions patients can take to reduce wait time. Here is a framework to organize your crafting of value-based guardrails.

- What is the top value you think must be honored to achieve your focus? What are four more? For example, you might pick "fairness to all." Do you need more values?
- If these five core values were converted into playground guidelines, how would they sound? A playground guideline might sound like "no hitting or backbiting."
- Pick an object that can represent your guardrail. For instance, for fairness to all, you might select a justice scale.
- If you were describing each guardrail to an eight-year-old, how would it sound? Write a short one-paragraph script that incorporates all five.
- What are three examples of what violations of this guardrail might look like in your partnerships?

Guardrails are value-based expectations that ensure borders with principles and protocols, with joint commitment. Agreements are the work expectations of the partnership. One reflects the code of conduct; one communicates the collaboration work promises. Guardrails guide the interpersonal relationship, whereas work agreements guide the productivity of the relationship. We will later explore crafting working agreements in Secret 4: Trust.

Manage Your Partnerships "By Hand"

Home repair of a faucet required a customer to purchase a ¾-inch copper fitting. At the store, a friendly sales associate helped the customer locate the copper fittings bin, but there was only one loose, unpackaged ¾-inch fitting left in the bottom of the bin. Somehow their inventory had not been replenished. On the front of the bin was the price: $1.99. The customer took the item to the checkout counter and was told, “It has no item number.” He related to the cashier that the item was the only one left lying loose in a bin with a price of $1.99 on the front. She flatly refused to proceed with the transaction unless she had the item number.

The customer suggested she call back to the plumbing department. Her call summoned the friendly sales associate to come to register 13. The sales associate related the customer’s same story—a $1.99 item without a package loose in the bin. She again stonewalled, heatedly sending him back for what she required.

“How about you just charge me $5,” pleaded the customer. “I am in a hurry and we are holding up other customers in your line.” Then all within earshot got to hear the sound of rigidity squared.

“This cash register will not let me ring up this fitting unless there is an item number.”

Following partnership values fosters flow and progression.
Submitting to union rules fuels obedience and defiance.

Co-creation partnerships should not be stymied by administrative rulemaking and mechanical procedures. Instead, they should be buttressed by guardrails crafted by hand (and by heart). Guardrails are core values, moral expectations on which you agree. What if you together identified the values you want to guide your partnership and converted them to more imaginative forms? Courtesy could become “play nice,” honesty could be “cherry tree,” and timeliness could be “stopwatch.” Remember, it is the process of together crafting values that exalts and solidifies their importance. Find ways to make them memorable, public, and practical.

Co-creation partnerships are the workshops of idea entrepreneurs. They cannot be streamlined, mechanized, or effectively served in a drive-by fashion. They are the handiwork of principled toil in pursuit of noble ends. When the players bring the best of who they are, not just the best of what they do, the winds of ingenuity blow in their favor.

Nurture through Elasticity, Not Endurance

Elasticity is about buoyancy, the opposite of rigidity. Elastic relationships have shock absorbers. They expand and unfold in their acceptance; little bumps in the rocky road of relationship are absorbed without a glare or the spotlight of attention. And elasticity releases the governor on the zeal to be experimental and exploratory. Elastic relationships encourage elbow room rather than close inspection. They seek ways to open rather than a means to close. Instead of nitpicking details, co-creation partnerships work to roll with normal imperfections. Pursue a can-do, “the answer is ‘yes,’ what’s your question?” type of optimism.

A large paint company in Santa Monica shipped an industrial customer many cases of mislabeled paint. The customer was a home construction company that built housing developments. When they discovered the error, lots of their painters were left standing around with nothing to do, and the inspector was due the afternoon of the next day. The customer called the paint company and got a customer service rep with a partnership attitude and a knack for inviting customer imagination.

"We can run another paint run but it will take until tomorrow to complete it; we can check with another warehouse to see if they have the LDB324 you need but it will take several hours to get it to you, or perhaps you have another solution you could recommend." The customer suggested, "Maybe you have a very similar color." It proved to an ideal solution . . . discovered by the customer. And it came from a provider interested in a partnership with elasticity, not rigidity.

Back to the wedding shower. Miss Lena gave her awkward pronouncement of the Circle's verdict her best shot. Dr. Nancy Marie Rainey Bell is still the high-spirited, restless racehorse she was over fifty years ago. Sharing a relationship with her has taught me that tolerance belongs only in relationships without spirit. Put tolerance in a vigorous relationship and you have a recipe for ironhanded conflicts and energy wasted on minutiae. Partnership elasticity, on the other hand, stretches the relationship so it can breathe, grow, and expand. It provides a playground for experimentation and flow. And partners who flow together, innovate together.

Construct Value-Based Guardrails: The Partnering Crib Notes

Take the sharp edges off conversations with your customer. Substitute being effective for being right. Agree on the values that guide your work, not the rules. Instead of "no interruptions during discussions," try "be kind and courteous." Replace typical meeting management rules with language more conducive to communicating that imagination is accepted and expected. Agendas become maps, parking lot becomes valet parking, and meeting notes become secret diaries. Invite outsiders to make appearances. What could a mime, a magician, an inventor, or an artist do for your gatherings? In the world of innovation, wacky wins; logical loses. In the world of co-creation partnerships, improvisation trumps organization. Make your gatherings feel like a jazz group extemporizing off of each other, not like a school glee club at contest. Make it like ad-libbing, not following a script. Discipline your collaboration with a porous hedge, not an iron-clad wall. Principle-centered boundaries can rein in without becoming the centerpiece; regulation-centered borders divert creative energy to limits and confines.

Co-creation partnerships are not undisciplined free-for-alls. Empowered ignorance is anarchy. The context of business already has a built-in innovation regulator. No one complains that a business solution is "just too darn logical." But let it be a bit on the wild, untested side, and the subtle retardants come out of the woodwork. Methodical is predictable; imaginative is a surprise. Reasonable is a popular feature of good solutions; outrageous gets raised eyebrows. Remember the premise behind brainstorming: it is easier to tone down than to think up. Let your co-creation partnership run free in the wild meadow of originality; it will be fenced in the stable of practicality soon enough.

It's a lot more difficult when the task ahead is not quite the same as what you've done before. When wayfinding is required. That's a different skill. That's the skill of finding the common threads, seeing the analogies and leaping over the crevices.

—SETH GODIN

CHAPTER 6

Be the Partnership Warranty

Responsibility changes everything. The moment we decide that we are the ones who are capable of and responsible for changing things, everything shifts.

—JOHN B. IZZO

"If you don't love it, sir, I'll buy it back from you!"

I stopped at the Farmview Market in Madison, Georgia, a few miles from my home—they specialize in homegrown produce and products from locals. I was on the hunt for a spicy sauce to use as a mop when grilling baby back ribs. The person who waited on me recommended Judge Cline's No. 9 sauce produced by a sauce maker a few miles away. When I expressed concern the sauce might have ingredients that could keep me awake at night, he uttered the opening line of this chapter. It was a rare "I *am* the warranty" moment.

"I *am* the warranty" is a clever caption for a T-shirt. Yet living an "I am accountable" attitude in relationships is a whole different matter. "I *am* the warranty" screams the unmistakable message that the buck stops with me. It trumpets to your customers, "I will personally take full responsibility for championing your request or need, and I will remain in total charge until your need is met to your complete satisfaction." It is as rare as hen's teeth. Yet it is mission-critical in a co-creation partnership.

Help Your Partner "Own" the Partnership

A friend attended a wedding for a relative. When it came time for the bride and groom to exchange their wedding vows, the minister turned first to the groom. It started the usual way: "Samuel, will you take Sharon to be your lawful wife . . ." Then the minister added to the "in sickness and in health" part the line "Will you take full responsibility for this marriage?" My friend's first reaction was to think it was the olden days when the man was head of the household and the little wife's primary role was to "obey."

But then the minister turned to the bride and repeated the exact same vows, complete with the "full responsibility" part. My friend was relieved we were still in the twenty-first century. He later would relate the powerful sentiment expressed in those vows. What if both parts in a relationship took full accountability? What if they both thought, "I *am* the warranty; the buck stops with me"?

Think of the confidence that would come if you never had to worry a second about partner abandonment or deliberate actions that would jeopardize the longevity of the relationship. Consider the bravery that could emanate from that kind of solid foundation. Most customer relationships are temporary, with a focus on scarcity; co-creation partnerships focus on abundance, whereby giving takes precedence over scorekeeping. And this attitude is about more than just fair dealings. It is fundamentally an expression of grace.

John Patterson and I have partnered for years on projects and assignments and even coauthored three books. We made a pact many years ago that sounded like this: You never have to wonder if I am privately angry or irritated at you. You never have to read my nonverbals and be concerned they reflect a subtle blaming message. If I am cross or peeved at you, you will know it. So if you experience me in a bad-tempered mood, never worry that the subject might be you if I have not told you. Did we have angry moments? Of course. But there was never pouting or smoldering irritation. Once we worked through an interpersonal skirmish, we moved ahead as a productive, happy partnership.

"I own the place" is more than a statement of proprietorship pride; it is a clarion call for buck-stopping. Years ago, when my wife and I borrowed money for a second home, there was a three-way telephone call between me, the representative of the title company, and the loan officer from Merrill Lynch. The title company representative kept demanding our loan officer talk with someone at Merrill about this essential or that requirement. Finally, the Merrill Lynch loan officer assertively told the title company rep, "I *am* Merrill Lynch." Long silence followed. "Oh," said the title company rep meekly, completely surrendering her accusatory attitude.

The attitude behind this kind of stance is one of accountability; it is also an orientation of culpability, as in "I will take the hit." When applied to a co-creation partnership, it is an invitation to jointness and a plea for oneness. Actions look like bold assertions, vibrant safeguards, and a dogged determination to make it work, and work well. Give to your partnership the best that you have; the best will come back to you.

Be the Net of Inspiration under Your Partnership High Wire

The emergence of your customer's imagination requires a safe landing and a protective context. Think of them as being like a parent in a pool encouraging a child's first plunge into the water with the words "Don't worry, I got you!" With that assurance, most children courageously jump into the deep end before they can swim. Before the invention of children's water wings, it was a giant leap of faith. Words help; attitude and action do even more. And the "I *am* the warranty" attitude personified looks like proactivity, caretaking, defending, and championing. It can be providing your customer with fairness choices that promote egalitarian behavior. When my sister or brother and I had to split a candy bar, we had a fairness process: whoever cut or broke the candy bar in half got to choose their half second.

One powerful way to be the full-warranty net for the high-wire, take-a-risk side of your partnership is to be an inspiration to your customer. One of the most innovative trapeze acts in the Ringling Bros. and Barnum & Bailey circus is the daring performance of the "Candelabra," where nine women hang in the air by their hair. On one occasion, an O-ring snapped and they all fell to the ground. Fortunately, they all lived. When circus performer and aerialist Elaine Alcorn was interviewed by CNN, she commented that nothing is ever fail-safe. Circus performers know they work in a high-risk world. But then she made the following comment . . . a powerful rationale for the power of inspiration on the path of innovation.

"They don't call it death defying for nothing. As a circus performer it is our job to do the impossible, to stare death in the face and conquer it," Alcorn said, adding that it's not all about the thrills. "We don't just do it for entertainment. We do it to inspire people, to inspire them to conquer their own fears or overcome their own obstacles. If you are the office worker and you have a deadline or trying to make ends meet or feed your hungry children, whatever your obstacles are, you can come to the circus and be reminded that nothing is impossible."[1]

Showing up to inspire places you in a special spirit of greatness. It telegraphs you care about influencing your partner to embrace the same orientation. More than self-talking your way to invincibility, it is a signal to all around you that you came to innovate. Invite your customer to take risks in the pursuit of inspired innovation, and be your customer's net when they step onto that high wire.

Accountability has two sides: "you can count on me" and "there will be an accounting." Both require promises that need to be kept.

Always Communicate You Really, Really Care

Customers too often get served by people focused on their task like an item on a checklist, instead of someone who understands the customer's goal and champions its achievement by caretaking it all the way to the end. Co-creation partnerships require that same type of proactive advocacy. It is more than taking care of your customer; it is taking care of your relationship by being an activist for its cause. It is wall-to-wall, end-to-end caring.

Discover is a large credit card company. My friend Shep Hyken, author of *The Convenience Revolution*, had an opportunity to present a series of customer service speeches at the customer support centers. To prepare, he visited the support center to listen and observe reps at work. One impressive area was collections, which Discover had smartly put in customer service and support. Shep watched reps talk with customers who had missed a payment. They showed empathy and concern for their customers as they discussed why the payment was missed. Some customers were willing to share reasons; others were less open. But that did not deter the reps from taking charge of the conversation to uncover an amicable solution.[2]

The Discover reps were helping customers generate mutually agreeable ways to handle a sensitive situation, and they were doing it with tact, diplomacy, and grace. Most of all, they were demonstrating a commitment to helping customers discover (pun intended) a creative solution, not just a pay-a-past-due-bill outcome. What could have been an adversarial situation became a partnership as the Discover support reps worked with their customers to come up with a payment solution that would make everyone happy.

Use "we" instead "I" and "you" whenever possible. Take time to listen, take care to understand, and take responsibility for the relationship. Be complimentary and affirming in your tone and language at a level that reflects your true feelings honestly conveyed to the customer. Be your customer's sponsor, as well as his or her advocate. Turn credit to your customer at every opportunity. Keep anchoring your discussion to the ultimate focus. Be gracious in your hosting and thoughtful in your remembering.

Focus on Your Customer, Not on the Procedures

Loyalty to a great laptop computer got totally trashed by a lousy replacement part! And this is a computer company from whom I had purchased several laptops. But I am getting ahead of myself.

I bought a new laptop and immediately ordered a backup power pack—one for the office and one for the road! The cord that goes from the wall outlet to the power pack arrived in a couple of weeks. But I learned the power pack with the cord to plug into the laptop was on back order. A call one month later was met with the same response—on back order.

Two months out, another call, same answer. Three months out, another call, same answer. But April and May were super busy, and I did not call. Not, that is, until an emergency happened. I was on a three-day client engagement and discovered I had accidentally left my only power pack in the office. A colleague suggested I check with the local Radio Shack. Miraculously, they had a universal in stock, and it worked perfectly. I also learned it was an item they had been carrying for a couple of years.

I made one more call to the computer company—now five months after the replacement part had been ordered—to cancel the order. But the "bad boy" in me came out during the call. "If I gave you personally one million dollars to come up with a solution to my power pack problem," I asked the parts clerk, "what could you recommend?" His answer: "I would have given you the tracking number so you could check on the back order yourself."

I was stunned. But I was not finished. "Were you aware that Radio Shack had a universal power pack for this particular laptop?" I asked curtly. "Yes, I was," he replied, "but we cannot guarantee their parts." I made one last lunge with my complaint sword. "So, you let me go five months waiting on a part that probably will never come because of *your* guarantee policy? What about customer service?"

"Is there anything else I can help you with today?" he asked.

The parts clerk-spokesperson for this well-known, global computer company focused exclusively on "the part" and not "the customer." He could say with great confidence that he had "done all his tasks" perfectly. Professor Levitt would say, "All the 'drill bits' were counted as my 'hole' was disregarded." Despite my affection for the laptop and its predecessors, my next one would be a different brand. Customers don't want providers that complete tasks—even if they do it perfectly. They want solutions. And innovating with customers should be solution focused, not task fixated.

Be the Partnership Warranty: The Partnering Crib Notes

You give your customers great security when you demonstrate you are deeply committed to their welfare. It is all the little things you do in a partnership that add up to demonstrable commitment. While we all know relationships can't always be a perfect 50-50 split, good relationships have a kind of floating reciprocity—some days 60-40, other days 40-60. People in relationships believe there will be an "it will all balance out in the end" type of fairness. But what if you inspired accountability from your partner by assuming responsibility for all of it, not just your half? When we lead with a search for absolute fairness, we also start with a scorekeeping orientation.

Partner with abundance, not reciprocity. Think of it as the "lover" standard of care. It would mean never giving up on your partner, and hanging in there through thick and thin, for better or for worse. It would mean going all in.

A Look Ahead: Discovery

We have started to unpack the process of getting inside your customer's imagination. A way to consider it is this: there are two approaches to your quest, invitation and attraction. Invitation revolves around who you are (curious, trustworthy, and passionate); attraction revolves around what you do (grounding and discovery). You have now explored an invitation approach in curiosity and an attraction approach in grounding. In the section to follow, another attraction is coming: how to use discovery and learning in a way that attracts your customer's imagination to come join you on the playground of ideas.

There are only two options regarding commitment: you're either in or you're out. There is no such thing as life in-between.

—PAT RILEY

Secret 3

DISCOVERY

Spark Daredevil Learning

Security is mostly a superstition.
Life is either a daring adventure or nothing.

—HELEN KELLER

Archeologists excavating the pyramids discovered wheat seeds that dated back to around 2500 BC. As in the tradition of antiquity, the seeds were there for the dead pharaoh to eat if he got hungry. The find was important because it would enable scientists to determine what variety of wheat was in use in the ancient world and could be invaluable for engineering new types of wheat.

Out of curiosity, the scientists planted the forty-five-hundred-year-old seeds in fertile soil and an amazing thing happened. They grew!

Innovation is the process of awakening, nurturing, and growing—just like the wheat seeds. Sometimes innovation is pure serendipity. Mark Twain wrote, "Name the greatest of all inventors. Accident." Some of my favorite accidents include Popsicles, potato chips, and Silly Putty. But most innovation—especially the kind that involves your customer's imagination—begins with an intentional pursuit. It is driven by a purpose but cultivated by a propensity to discover, to learn. If passion is the sunlight in the development of ideas, learning is its soil.

DISCOVERY

Together We Foster Risk-Taking

Your customer's imagination is deeply attracted to growth. Growth, like imagination, requires discovery and a daredevil-like confidence to let go of a fear of mistakes and embrace something new and different. Discovery, like imagination, involves tinkering around and experimenting, replacing old opinions with new truths. Secret 3 is about ramping up the attraction of mutual discovery as a means to draw out the imagination of your customer. Discovery embraces imagination like an old friend with a familiar history. There are fruitful ways to promote your customer's imagination's attendance at that reunion.

I grew up on a farm in South Georgia, where we grew corn and hay for our livestock. My dad always talked about the importance of rich topsoil. We planted cover crops in the winter to protect the topsoil from being washed away; when seeds were planted, we added fertilizer to enrich the topsoil. I remember as a child thinking that "rich" must mean there was treasure buried in the fields—I envisioned the gold, silver, and precious jewels that pirates pursued. While the form of my treasure was off the mark, my concept of nurturance for en-rich-ment was on target. Learning is a fertile, bountiful context for the growth of ideas.

Sometimes, the perfect combination of seed, soil, and weather would come together and we would get a bumper crop. The giant corn stalks would reach for the sky in a seemingly death-defying way. They would tower over all the other crops planted nearby. My father would tell me they were like a bunch of teenagers trying to outdo each other. He always animated the things we grew as though they had a spiritual life, not just an agronomic one.

"We have a bunch of daredevils," my father would tell my mother as he took off his farm hat that looked like a French-style pith helmet. "Hope we don't get hail before we get ears of corn." He seemed proud these cornstalks would take the risk to grow beyond their normal rank and pay grade. So it is with co-creation partnerships.

Learning requires the bravery to say, "I don't know," the humility to say, "I am open to being wrong," and the passion to say, "I am not letting setbacks inhibit my pursuit." Innovation takes daring to persevere despite criticism or rebuke. "When you innovate," said Oracle cofounder and executive chairman

Larry Ellison, "you've got to be prepared for everyone telling you that you're nuts." Co-creation partnerships are always learning and learning in out-of-the-ordinary ways.

Discovery is a forever feature of all innovation cultures. And it is a poignant attraction for your customer's imagination. It has three parts (figure 5). First, it involves helping your customer feel like a valued part of a coalition engaged in the incubation of ideas, a welcome arena for divergent views and irreverent perspectives. Second, it is about presence, a "be all . . . there" emotional place filled with animation, full attention, and wide-awake consideration. And finally, it is a context for imagination chi—a high-energy means to stretch the imagination in order to discover, invent, and originate.

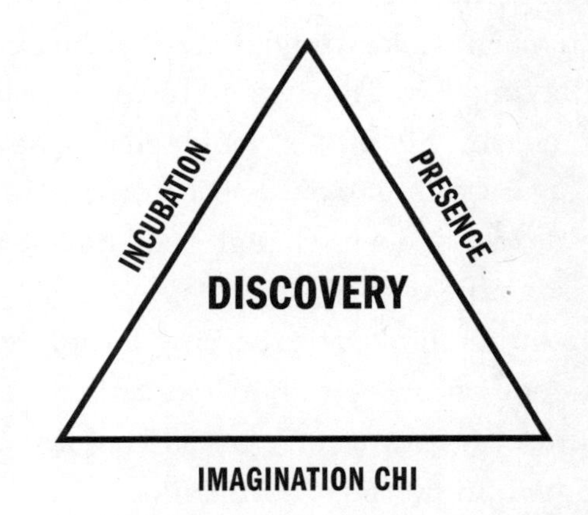

FIGURE 5. The elements of partnership discovery

Discovery, like imagination, is a door opened only from the inside. It starts with a context—an incubation alliance—that encourages door opening to allow your customer's imagination to exit. This is a cauldron fired up by obvious humility, laser-focused presence, and above all, freedom of expression. It is a relationship jam-packed with awe, wonderment, and the courage for full disclosure. It entails acknowledging and making room for what you do not know. And it requires exorcising anything that creates fear in the relationship.

Discovery fuels innovation when those involved are omnipresent, meaning they are emotionally present in all ways. I label it "be all . . . there." It means being "on" and remaining "on." It includes energizing by example. Athletes call it "leaving everything on the field or court." This cheerleader-for-learning orientation can awaken the imagination, getting it on the team bus bound for innovation.

Discovery sprouts ideas by stretching the imagination in new ways. Why do great athletes or acrobatic performers stretch before a contest or performance? The short answer is to loosen up their muscles so they are less likely to be injured. But the deeper answer is to invite the stimulation of chi—the Chinese word for life force or breath of life. Chi is what makes a live body different from a corpse. And a strong life force is associated with aliveness, alertness, and presence. Have you noticed runners or gymnasts shaking their hands before lunging into action? It is the body's relationship reaction to chi. For innovation, wise pursuers use special stretches to awaken the imagination.

In the three chapters ahead, we will unearth new concepts and practices in the creation of a climate of incubation and explore ways to bring "wide awakeness" to the relationship. We will also explore in an entertaining chapter how to stretch the spirit and practice of imagination with your customer. We have all heard the phrase "stretch of the imagination." What would that be like if it were the spirited version of a physical workout in the gymnasium of ideas?

So is it discovery or learning? The answer is “yes!” Some learning is rote and repetitive like the muscle memory of a dancer; some involves retention of facts and formulas like preparing for a high school test. These types of learning yield performance. But discovery-centered learning produces insights, inventions, and progress. It is treasure-hunting learning, not answer-knowing learning. Thus, the process of discovery and this type of learning are almost interchangeable.

CHAPTER 7

Create an Incubation Alliance

A successful imaginer has the imagination of a five-year-old with the wisdom of a grandparent.

—WALT DISNEY

My grandmother was an incubator. Near her backyard, she had a chicken house divided into a row of cubbies much like the ones you had in grade school. Each cubby had a floor of pine straw and a raw light bulb on top. It was where her chickens laid their eggs. I lived nearby, and when I visited my grandparents, my job was to empty the nest of eggs she would use for cooking. The hens did not seem to mind since they had plenty more on the way. However, when the goal was baby chickens instead of eggs, the light was turned on. And the hens were not at all amused at my territorial invasion.

My grandmother sang a lot to the chickens perched on their eggs. Her small garden was right beside the chicken house and she sang as she weeded or picked vegetables. I thought the process was magical when chicks (or "biddies" as we called them) pecked their way out of the eggshell. I remember wondering if it might have been my grandmother's singing that enticed them to leave the safety of their shell. Or was it the glow or heat of the raw light bulb positioned above them in their cubby? An incubation alliance feels to its participants like my grandmother's chicken house must have felt to her hens.

Generate a Rapport Retreat

An incubation alliance is an environment laced with conditions and dispositions that favor the birth of ideas. My grandmother's chicken yard was surrounded by a high chicken-wire fence designed to keep the hens in and the foxes out. It was physically safe. But a rapport retreat is less about physical conditions (colorful pictures, great music, or comfy seats) and more about the security of positive dispositions, affirming attitudes, and optimistic moods.

Why rapport? "Rapport" comes from an antique French word that means "harmony renewed." It is the expression we use to mean "establishing a safe connection." Most people approaching a potentially anxious encounter will raise their antennae high in search of clues about the road ahead: Will this situation embarrass me? Will this person take advantage of me? Will I be effective in this encounter? When I fail, will I be perceived as a failure?

What about the world inside your customer's imagination? It does not likely come streaming out just on its own. Unless your customer is a rare person, he or she does not go through the business day with a wild imagination set on full speed ahead. It comes out as needed, if at all. And it comes out by invitation through your interpersonal conduct, or it is attracted out, riding on the vehicle of an important cause or accompanied by its cousin, discovery. The secret you are about to explore is all about the anatomy, attributes, and applications of that cousin.

In the first secret we reviewed how to send an irresistible invitation to your customer's imagination through your curiosity manifested as eccentric listening, witnessing your customer, and unbiased inquiry. In the second secret we explored how to create a profound attraction through grounding, exhibited as a compelling focus, with helpful guardrails and full accountability for success. We will now begin our examination of another secret to attract your customer's imagination: discovery (read: learning). And it begins like most relationships, with establishing rapport.

The Arbor Company is a successful chain of senior living communities. Each community has an "Engagement" staff whose job is to involve residents in designing activities they will find enjoyable and that promote their overall health. Arbor created a contest among all their communities to enhance the Engagement programs in a uniquely innovative way. One successful program was called "Love it or Leave Us." The staff was challenged to assess what's happening in their communities during high-frequency new prospect tour times and to generate ideas for activities to be used during those times to help create prospect rapport by making their community feel more energized.

The program has had multiple beneficiaries: the residents, who have more activity opportunities; the staff, who have an enhanced involvement with residents (their customers); and the prospects, who see a more active environment and therefore may be more inclined to choose the Arbor community as being the right fit for them and thus "love it" rather than "leave us."

How do you create a rapport that connects? Use welcoming tones, bring a gift, create the excitement and anticipation of a birthday party, take time to get really acquainted—longer than you normally might. Create a spirit of openness and positive regard. Start with a fun topic. Add whimsy to the ambiance. Make your customer the center of attention. Talk about the future as opportunity, not challenge. Do something quirky to alter the status quo of an otherwise serious meeting in search of a serious solution. These are actions to add to the attraction; what are actions to avoid?

Stop Thinking It's Picture Day

Perfection is the enemy of excellence. Now don't get me wrong. There are clearly areas where perfection should be the minimum standard. If my surgeon is doing surgery on what's inside my skull or the pilot is landing the plane in which I am a passenger, I want absolutely zero defects—total perfection. No hospital would get away with a quality goal of a 99.9 percent accuracy rate on the number of dropped babies!

Discovery is not like hunting for Easter eggs with a colorful basket of fake straw;
discovery is like Indiana Jones's Ark of the Covenant hunting . . . with snakes!
There are risks.

The challenge with the pursuit of perfection (with a hat tip to our brain surgeon, pilot, and baby-dropping exceptions) is it can slow momentum or stop progress. While "good enough for government work" might signal an acquiescence to mediocrity, the standard my son Bilijack uses—"Hey, it's not picture day"—telegraphs that we do our very best and move on, not worrying about reaching perfection but enjoying the substance of excellence. To quote Norman Vincent Peale, "Shoot for the moon. Even if you miss, you end up among the stars."

Why is a picture-day mentality a problem? The application of imagination in an innovation setting needs a rough and tumble, sawdust-on-the-floor type of environment, not a sterilized, error-avoiding operating room. A push for perfection can lasso experimentation and pull it to the ground of inspection and close-up evaluation. It can stymie a make-it-up-as-we-go freedom that allows "tentative" to feel at home and "speculative" to be safe.

The CEO of a senior living company announced to her leadership group they would be holding a retreat at a rustic venue instead of the "big conference room," as they called it. "Wear jeans," she told the group. "Not your nice jeans you wear to an outdoor party, I mean the worn-out pair you wear to paint. Tomorrow, we will be wallowing in wild ideas and we need to focus on imagination, not on formality." It was her way of saying, "This is not picture day."

Help your customer lighten up, let go, kick back, and save perfection for a rare picture day. Eliminate emotional barriers. Build an out-of-the-box activity into your meeting plan, and early. Meet in fun places, not a formal meeting room. Turn mistakes into fun learnings to celebrate rather than criticize. One company gives a "green wiener" award to the person who makes the biggest mistake (while doing their best) that results in valuable learning for all. Assume that orientation with your customer. Confucius said: "Better a diamond with a flaw than a pebble without."

Imagination is more attractive when dressed in work clothes. For your customers, it means an environment of "we can be a bit wacky," "let's have fun," and "this will lead to something novel." It is a setting where judgment waits in the next room until summoned. However, such refereeing of the relationship is in your hands as the provider. Stay vigilant for any sights, sounds, and scenarios that signal judgment and criticism have escaped their confinement to infiltrate your relationship.

Enroll Together in Daredevil Learning

Let's have fun with a simulated example. You are the owner of a large printing company. Your reputation is built on high-quality printing, lightning fast responsiveness, and a willingness to pull out all the stops to meet your customers' needs. Customers bring or email you what they need printed, a proof is prepared for their review, it is printed on approval, and a local courier is used to deliver the finished goods. One of your most prominent customers is a very large resort community. Their head of operations wants even faster turn time on print jobs without sacrificing quality. She has ideas and schedules a meeting with you to discuss her need. Here are a few daredevil principles to guide your discussion.

- Find expert input that can enable you and your customer to learn together. Not just best practices, new practices you can observe or hear about.
- Schedule your meeting at your customer's location to gain a deeper understanding of the context of his or her need.
- Start your meeting by brainstorming all the ways the key variable (in this case, speed) can be interpreted (e.g., agility instead of pace).
- Identify ways this key variable is operationalized in other contexts (e.g., electronically, drones, embedded devices, and so forth).
- Look at your customer's need from new angles (e.g., if your product could speak, what would it suggest?).

Create Unmistakable Acceptance

Co-creation partnerships are girded by complete acceptance. Accepting means encouraging your customer to be courageous enough to take the risks needed to unfreeze old habits and embrace new practices. It is the trumpeting of support, despite unstable first attempts and timid trials. It means helping your customer feel like a full owner, not a tenant or junior partner.

Ownership also matters when you are in search of product improvements. For example, how could you improve on a product as simple and pedestrian as a baby bottle? Playtex, Evenflo, and Similac have all tweaked the hundred-year-old design with better nipples, easier handles, and ways to minimize uncomfortable air intake. But Jason Tebeau took the baby bottle in a completely different direction.

It all started when Jason's mom was babysitting. Driving with a child in the car seat in the passenger seat, she got frustrated having to stop the car to reposition the baby bottle and stop the child from crying. Jason learned other parents had the same frustration with baby bottles—they were operationally parent dependent. He created a hands-free bottle that left the baby independent during feeding time. But what he created is not the story; how he created it is a tutorial in ways to get inside your customer's imagination.

Assembling a group of fifty babies with parents in tow, Tebeau and the parents observed babies interacting with bottles in various stages of the design process as assorted product challenges were solved—how to work with the physics of liquid moving up a tube, how to capitalize on babies' tendencies to put everything in their mouth and treat every object as a toy, how to use a valve to retain liquid in the pacifier-style nipple so babies would not lose interest if they stopped sucking and the liquid fell back into the bottle. At each phase, he interviewed and brainstormed with parents and listened to them in focus groups talking to each other about what they had observed. They were treated as baby experts; he was simply a bottle designer.

The result of their collaboration was the popular Pacifeeder, one of several products from Tebeau's company Savi Baby. Sold at retail outlets like Target and Amazon, the bottle has been so well liked many babies prefer it over the traditional "lie in mommy's lap" variety. The customers—the babies and their parents—were intimately involved throughout. Tebeau even used parents to help him determine the appropriate price and conceive ideas for promoting his creative product, knowing retailers might see it as "just another baby bottle."[1] Notice the complete acceptance and obvious trust Tebeau placed in his customers. It is this attractive approval that makes customers want to share their imagination and claim the pride of co-creation.

The opportunity to co-create is a gift you give your customer as a way to summon their imagination. Orators start with a joke, salespeople start with chitchat rather than features and benefits, and you bring a bottle of wine to a dinner party. All these gifts signify that beginnings can be difficult. When the welcome mat of imagination is an opportunity to discover together, it attracts the customer's imagination to come out and add to the mix.

Create an Incubation Alliance: The Partnering Crib Notes

Turn everything into a learning challenge. So, why *is* the sky blue? Put on your hobby hat and consider new learning opportunities you and your customers could share. "I have never played __________; I understand you have not either. I would enjoy learning it with you." Watch a relevant TED talk together. Level the learning field by ensuring every effort is egalitarian without a hint of a schoolmarm-to-student gap. Turn your innovation gatherings into games or treasure hunts. Put learning points on coffee mugs, instructional information on bathroom walls. Write a blog together. Bring in visitors to introduce new angles regarding your customer challenge. If your challenge were a meal, what would it be like? Let's get a chef to prepare it. "Incubate" comes from the word "brood" meaning "to nurse." Nurse innovation by supporting the emotional environment in which it grows.

The late Hallmark Cards artist Gordon MacKenzie in his best-selling book *Orbiting the Giant Hairball* tells the story about his time volunteering as an artist-in-residence in the Kansas City-area elementary schools. When he entered a first-grade class, he would ask, "How many artists do we have here?" and all the children would raise their hands. The same question asked of third graders yielded only about half the number of raised hands. And when MacKenzie asked the sixth graders his question, only one or two "closet" artists would timidly raise their hands. What happened to youthful eagerness?[2] The goal of an incubation alliance is getting "all hands in the air."

There's a good reason Google puts ping-pong tables in their headquarters. If you want to encourage insights, you've got to also encourage people to relax.

—JOHN KOUNIOS, cognitive neuroscientist at Drexel University

CHAPTER 8

Be All . . . There

One person with passion is better than forty people merely interested.

—E. M. FORSTER

"All present and accounted for, sir!" It was the roll call response a platoon leader would give the military company commander to signal that no one in the platoon was absent and all soldiers were in formation. As an army platoon leader, I remember it was expected the phrase be spoken loudly and with authority . . . like a pledge or guarantee. Then I took over an army reconnaissance unit and the phrase had a new meaning.

My 82nd Airborne commander instructed his unit leaders to put an emphasis on the word "present." It was an emotional roll call that communicated the entire unit was in their most gung ho, "warrior" frame of mind and ready for combat. They were not just "there" as in present, they were "all there." As a recon unit leader in an airborne command, you were not expected to just round up the troops for formation; you were expected to inspire them to be ready to make something happen. "Be all" as in "the most you could be"; "be there" as in emotionally present.

"Be all . . . there" is a condition for the kind of learning that attracts imagination and leads to innovation. Co-creation partnerships that are wide awake have an everlasting energy and intensity in every encounter. They are never lazy or indifferent; when they are there, they are all there. In conversations, they are attentive—showing curiosity when they listen, animation when they contribute. My consulting firm has a norm when working with clients: "We don't do tired." We might be tired, but the customer would never know it. It is a way to show respect. Done consistently, it attracts your customer to jump off the high dive, so to speak.

Being all . . . there means personally being an assertive learner. Harvard professor Rosabeth Moss Kanter said, "Leaders are more powerful role models when they learn than when they teach." It also means assertively helping your customer continually learn. It includes staying on the hunt for obvious and subtle ways to foster informal learning.

Hardwire Learning into Your Partnership

Informal learning is finding nontraditional ways to infuse learning into every fiber of the experience. Here is an example. My business partner and I were working with a company that owned and managed hundreds of shopping malls around the country. The company had asked us to help them determine if creating a great experience in their malls would drive traffic into the retail stores, raising store revenue. The company earned its revenue in two ways—they charged rent to mall retailers, and they took a percentage of the retail sales brought in by the mall stores. So they had a mutual interest in store revenue. They knew they could put a circus in the mall and raise the car count in the parking lot; the challenge was whether the traffic that came into the mall actually went into the stores and spent money.

They smartly realized mining customers' imaginations would be important to finding a solution that the target market would enjoy. Four pairs of malls were selected for the test. Each pair had very similar metrics. One in each pair would be the control mall at which nothing was done to change the mall experience. The other was the experimental mall at which a unique mall theme and experience was designed to match the target customer group and fashioned to drive increased traffic into the mall stores. The ideation sessions were held at the Catalyst Ranch, an amazing innovation center in Chicago.

Several meetings enabled them to ensure high-energy learning was woven throughout the all-day sessions. There was a fun homework assignment. The session goal was posted, written both in boardroom language and how kids might say it. There were cool sayings on the wall and customer data on giant posters that showed a prism of psychographic and sociographic information about the target market (e.g., what customers liked in movies, TV programs, retailers, books, social activities, and so forth). There were giant photos of customers and store personnel interacting. Unique meals and snack breaks were creatively displayed and managed with learning in mind. Distinctive toys, hats, and manipulatives were everywhere. The table was set for discovery. At the end of the long day, a common theme from both company personnel and customers was how much they had learned about each other and how much they looked forward to the follow-up.

Let's look at this co-creation example up close. Provider and customers learned together. They were clear about the focus from the outset. They worked as equals, not as subjects in an experiment. They combined fact-based data with innovative experiences. They held their ideation session off site at a place designed for R&D-like events. They clothed the entire setting with out-of-the-box artifacts, right down to quirky menu items. They came prepared. They made it fun and exciting, stimulating all the senses in the process. They kept it from becoming a one-and-done experience. Every component was choregraphed to ensure attendees were deeply and completely engaged. And there was amazing discovery as a result.

Grow from a Nothing-Is-Impossible Attitude

Necessity is the mother of invention. And necessity can be real peril at the door or the basis for a firefighter-in-training attitude. Such a stance creates self-assurance that encourages your customer's imagination to join and engage. Let's examine a real story.

Harley-Davidson was on the brink of bankruptcy, after years as a cult-like brand. Japanese bike makers Honda, Suzuki, and Kawasaki along with German giant BMW were entering the domestic market in the 1960s, eating deeply into Harley's market share. The newcomers were giants with deep pockets; Harley had heritage and mystique, features hard to put on a bank deposit slip. AMF bailed them out by purchasing the company. Harley's quality suffered as AMF pushed the company into aggressive overproduction. Then in the unkindest cut of all, AMF replaced the iconic Harley brand name with its own. Survival of one of the world's most renowned brands was unlikely.

Harley turned to its customers. Willie G. Davidson, the grandson of one of the founders and the sixty-four-year-old head of the design department, donned a black jacket and beret and took to the road on his Harley to meet with customers across the country to honestly relate Harley's challenge and plead for their help. Customers wanted the old motorcycle models with the outlaw flourishes that turned Harleys into "choppers." And they were willing to help promote the brand. Returning from his learning trip, Willie G. designed all new lines, like the Softail, which mimicked the style and classic elegance of the 1940s Hydra Glide.

They also in 1983 established the Harley Owners Group (HOG). Twenty-eight people came to the first bike rally. Today there are over a million members and Harley-Davidson is a success story. And the company continues to push what retired CEO Rich Teerlink called "unfinished finished products," aftermarket products for owners to customize their bikes.[1]

Access to inside your customer's imagination comes with learning and discovering together, out loud. Harley knew its customers treasured the colorful legacy of their storied brand. So the ambassador they sent was more of a missionary than a corporate spokesperson; he was someone who could relate, rally, and recruit the heart and soul of customers. They also knew customers had to be the centerpiece of their resurrection.

When I was an instructor in their Harley-Davidson University for dealerships, the most sacred closed meeting was between corporate leaders and the Harley dealers' council. Old-timers referred to this unique gathering as prayer meeting, a forum for the two-way learning of the unvarnished truth. No surprise that Harley-Davidson was a key prototype example in Peter Senge's book *The Fifth Discipline* on how to become a learning organization.[2]

"If you want something to grow, pour champagne on it," said Carol Lavin Bernick, former chair of skin care manufacturer Alberto-Culver. It means giving more than you think you can to your customer's challenge. Marketing guru Seth Godin is fond of asking audiences to "hold up your hand in the air as high as you can." Once the audience complies, he says, "Now, hold it up a little bit higher." Everyone in the audience complies with the bit more they were holding back. "What's up with that?" asks Godin. "What kept you from giving it all you had on the first request?"[3]

Be all . . . there means starting with a champagne effort right out of the blocks. It means assuming you can do the impossible. It entails holding your hand as high as you can right out of the gate. Remember, you'll still wind up in the stars.

Tune into the Discovery Channel

Pretend you are the head of marketing for a small chain of funeral homes. A group of ministers, key customers who refer families to your funeral homes, are concerned that a growing number of families are abandoning the church as the site for funerals and instead using local restaurants or country clubs. Many families design and conduct their own services without a minister. The ministers have scheduled a meeting with you to voice their concerns and discover solutions that benefit the churches as well as your business. Here are a few questions to organize your meeting.

- **Look up:** What is a grander, nobler vision for your customer's need or aspiration?
- **Look back:** What has history taught you about this type of need?

* **Look around:** How are winners in similar circumstances dealing with this type of challenge?
* **Look out:** What are potential potholes you need to avoid as you consider wild ideas?
* **Look in:** What is your role and opportunity to transform your customer's dream into a dream come true?

If you had the capacity to put a QR code anywhere you wanted, linked to any learning resource you wanted, where would you put it and what would be the resource? If you could invite any expert on the planet to help your partnership learn something new related to your customer's challenge, who would it be?

Practice Never-Give-Up Tenacity

Pitney Bowes Global Mailing Solutions was transforming from commodity-based to solution-based sales. It required sales VPs to think, act, and lead like general managers. My friend Dave Basarab, education director at that time, decided to hold a two-day event called The Executive Challenge. The goal was to jump-start the change initiative by having the target audience understand and embrace the new business strategy and develop a "general manager mindset."

Dave chose to use a business simulation to train all 120 people at the same time. His boss hated simulations, but Dave convinced him this one would be different; it would be customized to the population, teach the new strategy, and develop the necessary leadership skills. His boss reluctantly agreed; Dave realized he was betting his job on this one event. But there was another hurdle.

The technology to simultaneously run 120 students through an online business simulation customized to their needs did not exist. Dave needed a partner to create one and help run a world-class experience. He chose Enspire Learning, a boutique start-up firm from Austin, Texas. No one had ever done this before, including Enspire. Dave soon realized Enspire was betting their company on the project. For months the two teams worked, not as customer and vendor, but as a partnership. There were moments when thought was given to "sitting this one out." But their tenacity to hang in there to the end kept them going.

When the day came to run The Executive Challenge, they had twelve classrooms, one for each division, running the simulation jointly facilitated by one of Dave's team members, a member from Enspire, and the sales VP. Enspire wired the classrooms to their server housed in Dave's facility staffed by half a dozen programmers. Each division competed against the other divisions. They could see in real time how they performed to target and against the other divisions. The Executive Challenge was a huge success—end-of-event ratings were the highest they had ever achieved, and the twelve-month ROI was 220 percent. Dave Basarab got to keep his job and earned the admiration of his boss, the event won an award for best use of innovation, Dave's company was listed in *Training* magazine's Top 100, and Enspire Learning went on to become a very successful company.

Recall the cartoon of a heron on a river bank with the head of a frog in its mouth? The frog has its front legs wrapped around the throat of the heron, preventing it from swallowing. The caption reads: Never, ever give up! Show that attitude in your partnership!

 Be All . . . There: The Partnering Crib Notes

Show up for meetings ten minutes early. Take notes, even if you don't plan to read or keep them. Just the notetaking process will increase what you learn, remember, and have available to use. Include in your customer innovation sessions a mini-lesson on an interesting topic. Be the instructor; let your customer be the instructor. Post clever sayings related to the customer challenge on the walls in your meeting room. Add cartoons to your exploration. Invite your customer to a business conference related to your focus. Search related articles and blogs and share them. Together volunteer for an important cause you both value. Add a "what'd we learn" component to all debriefs and postmortems. Add a learning metric to assess your collective performance.

Texas Bix Bender, the author of *Don't Squat with Yer Spurs On!*, wrote in that book, "A body can pretend to care, but they can't pretend to be there."[4] When Bender wrote the line, the message was about the opposite of absent. But true caring is not about "present and accounted for." It does not mean making a meeting, or attending a function, or occupying a chair. It means the army recon version—bringing your heart, soul, and every ounce of your "very best." Get up, dress up, show up, and never give up!

We entered school as question marks,
but graduated as periods.
—JOHN HOLT

CHAPTER 9

Stretch Imagination Chi

True success is achieved by stretching oneself, learning to feel comfortable being uncomfortable.
—KEN POIROT

Every time our cat, Gypsy, wakes from one of her many long naps, her first action is to stretch. "As a cat stretches," says Andrew Cuff, a researcher at the Royal Veterinary College in London, "it activates all of their muscles and increases their blood pressure, which increases the amount of blood flowing to the muscles and also to the brain. This helps wake cats up and makes them more alert."[1] Since her stretches look a lot like Tai Chi movements, we wonder if she is balancing her chi!

Wide awake and alert (be all . . . there) is a crucial part of an effective co-creation partnership. It creates an animation or vivaciousness that stirs ideas to a boil, making them hot for application. Half-baked becomes ready to serve. Think of this chapter as your recipe for relationship exercises aimed at getting the creative juices going while invigorating the relationship with your customer. It is an appetizer for discovery.

The imagination door your customer controls is a lot like the lid to a jack-in-the-box. Decorated to entertain, the toy plays music as the crank is turned. The timing of the emergence of the creative, happy-go-lucky jack is a surprise, making its owner laugh. You can influence the turning of the crank by the enthusiasm of your attitude, the sincerity of your gratitude, and the aroma of your rabbit food. (I added that third rhyme just to make you smile.)

Stretch with Generosity

A student at Morehouse College was unable to find a babysitter for his five-month-old daughter. His wife had necessary chores, and he was studying for a midterm algebra exam. The class was to be a critical review. So he brought his child to the class at this all-male college in Atlanta. But it created a new problem—how to hold his baby and take notes. Professor Nathan Alexander volunteered to carry the child in his arms while he lectured and periodically wrote on the chalkboard.

"Stretch" and "generosity" can give the expression of abundance unexpected applications. Generosity elevates, ennobles, and enriches, causing the relationship to blossom and grow. Following the "holding the baby" incident, Morehouse College president David Thomas tweeted, "This is about love and commitment. Loving our students and being committed to removing any barrier to their pursuit of excellence."[2] The same could be said for attracting your customer's imagination.

"Innovation is guts plus generosity," wrote marketing guru Seth Godin. "Guts because it might not work. And, generosity because guts without seeking to make things better is merely hustle. The innovator shows up with something she knows might not work. Everyone else has been trained to show up with a proven, verified, approved, answer that will get them an A on the test. If failure is not an option, most of the time, neither is success. Allow generosity to take the lead and you'll probably discover that it's easier to find the guts."[3]

A high-tech distributor and one of their major transportation vendors held a problem-solving meeting. The goal was to figure out a new way to accommodate large- and small-batch loads on the same route. The distributor was concerned about turn time for shipments to customers; the vendor was concerned about the cost created by additional stops for small batches with a lower ROI. When the facilitator learned the vendor and distributor were headquartered in the same area, he suggested a novel start to their meeting. "Let's begin by brainstorming how together we can help provide kids with more well-lit play zones other than the limited parks we have in the Muddywater area." It changed the tone of the gathering from "what about me?" to "what about us?" It also hastened the breakthrough both parties sought.

Be willing to assist your customer with a chore that might normally be theirs to do. It sounds like, "I'll help you set up." Bring or send something that might be of interest to your customer: "I read this article about a new program at Duke, and I remembered your daughter is going to college there next year." Remember important milestones and red-letter days. Look for any reason to make a big deal out of the week, the day, or the hour. A friend told me he turned a customer into a partner when his customer inquired about a book on the credenza behind his desk. My friend told his customer, "Take it with you. I've already read it!" Make random acts of kindness frequent acts and notice their impact on the quality of the relationship.

Stretch with an Imagination Appetizer

Stretching your body does not start with a ground-pounding strenuous workout, it begins with low impact stretches and evolves to stronger ones. Imagination needs an appetizer. And the best kinds of appetizers follow the rules of an effective climate-setting exercise in a training class. They need three features: guarantee success (never use it to show what one doesn't know), make it relate to the subject of your customer's need, and make its form fit the nature of the innovation workout you plan with your customer.

Walk into a theatre for a Broadway play in New York and the appetizer you are given between the ticket counter and your seat is the Playbill. It not only is a tool to tell you about the plot and characters, it sets the mood for what you are about to see and hear. Walk into an upscale restaurant and you are likely to get something "compliments of the chef," a tasty appetizer preparing you for the meal you have just ordered. My car dealership makes sure there are a couple of hazelnut (my favorite) K-Cups at their Keurig machine when I go for maintenance or service and spend time in their waiting area.

McLane is a large wholesale supply company headquartered in Temple, Texas, that distributes grocery and nonfood items to convenience stores. They are currently owned by Berkshire Hathaway. When I worked with their leadership group in 2000, the meeting was led by Terry McElroy, then head of operations. He opened their meeting with prayer, they did a fun creativity exercise ("Turn a bad idea like blue jeans for garbage cans or egg-flavored toothpaste into a benefit and make a quick sales pitch"), and then they all stood and gave the company cheer. I remember it as one of the most animated leadership meetings I had ever attended. I learned it was a climate-setting pattern they used for every leadership meeting. Appetizers get you ready for the innovation entrée.

Stretch with Storyboarding

The storyboard of the customer's experience or use of a product is a detailed plan of the structure of the experience—frame by frame, so to speak. Storyboarding is the process of experience choreography. It considers every tiny angle, from curb appeal to first impressions to the management of all the elements (tone and style, sight and sound) that impact the customer's experience and memory of the story. The intent is to alter or enhance the customer's sense of reality. It enables all elements—space, time, and physical objects—to be a cohesive, integrated whole. The Greeks called it scenography, having everything in the composition of a play working together to create a seamless, congruent experience for everyone in the theatre.

Airbnb is the largest lodging company in the world, with over seven million lodging sites in over one hundred thousand cities. In his book *Competing Against Luck: The Story of Innovation and Customer Choice*, Clay Christensen and his coauthors describe how Airbnb founders storyboarded forty-five different emotional moments for Airbnb hosts (people willing to rent out a spare bedroom or their entire house) and their guests. Together, these storyboards made up a mini-documentary of the experiences. CEO Brian Chesky told *Fast Company*, "Are these hosts men or women? Are they young or old? Where do they live, the city or countryside? Why are they hosting? Are they nervous? Are their guests arriving tired? At that point you start designing for stuff for a very particular use case."[4]

Part of imagination chi is seeking new angles for stretching the imagination. Like all innovation, it is seeing what everyone else is seeing but thinking what no one else is thinking.

Edward de Bono in his book *Lateral Thinking* describes how the pneumatic jack that telescopes up from the middle was imagined when its inventor carefully watched the back end of a cow in the process of defecating![5]

Stretch with More Answers

It was a typical weekly staff meeting at the Harvey Hotel in Plano, Texas. At one point in the second half of the meeting, hotel general manager John Longstreet announced that two guests had been invited to join the staff meeting for the "What's Stupid" portion.

Once they were introduced, Longstreet shared with the two guests instructions his staff already knew. "Every week we devote time in our staff meeting to hearing what's stupid around here. It teaches us a lot about how to get better. It also is a way to find new answers to old questions. We need your help. My job is to take notes and listen! After the meeting we all go to work making this hotel the very best it can be. We believe the answers to all our challenges and opportunities are always in the room."

What followed was a lively, no-holds-barred session about the little things that got in the way of delivering world-class guest service. Reserved initially, the two guests were soon chiming in with their observations and suggestions. The meeting was upbeat, not negative; it was supportive, not derisive. And there was not an inkling of fear in the room. The popular mantra that peppered the meeting was "two more ideas." Regardless of the topic or success of the discussion, there was constant team encouragement for "two more ideas." Many of the most creative insights came from the "two mores."

"There is hidden brilliance in every staff," Longstreet told me in an interview later. "The key is to create an environment that allows that brilliance to surface and shine." Innovation unleashed can come only from a partner unleashed. Brilliant answers are always in the room, often found on the other side of "two more ideas."

Stretch Imagination Chi: The Partnering Crib Notes

Imagination chi is all about juicing up the process with many versions of "what if." What if you had two more ideas, added special comfort, provided more generosity, created more flourishes, or invented more stories? What would your customer challenge or issue be like if you had a magic wand and could change one important aspect about it? What if you had unlimited resources or were a superhero with supernatural powers? What if you approached the situation with the goal of making it completely different from any other on the planet? What if the solution were going to carry the name of your child, your parents, your customer's child? What if it is a "let's pretend" game that summons your customer's imagination to join in? It works because it is an imagination-stretching exercise by definition. Let your imagination chi run wild like a kid getting off the school bus on the last day of school.

A Look Ahead: Trust

Our last two secrets for getting inside your customer's imagination have focused on attraction, amplifying the draw power of their features. The secrets Grounding and Discovery are like enticements so compelling that the imagination in your customer cannot wait to come out and play. The next secret returns to an invitation-like appeal. Trust is a manifestation of who you are more than what you do. In this section we will explore the importance of telling the truth, the value of clear work agreements, and how to plan for times when hiccups occur.

Breakthroughs come from an instinctive judgment of what customers might want if they knew to think about it.

—ANDREW GROVE, FORMER CEO OF INTEL

Secret 4

TRUST

Pursue Truth, Justice, and the Imagination Way

A relationship with no trust is like a cell phone with no service; all you can do is play games.

—UNKNOWN

Honor wine. It is a signature feature of Vincenzo's Ristorante in Omaha, Nebraska. The wait staff at Vincenzo's greet patrons at their table with a pitcher of their "honor wine"—an excellent Chianti. "Enjoy this if you like," the waitress said to a group of us. "We charge by the glass. At the end of the meal just let me know how many glasses you had and I'll add it to your bill." When I asked the owner on our way out how many patrons drink the Chianti, he smiled and said, "Most . . . it's one of our best features!"

Your customer's imagination resides in a cocoon of emotional defense. Brain specialists inform us that every time a person is presented with a problem or a challenge, their imagination (right brain) provides a quiet answer or idea for a solution. But we hear only the loud response of our logical, rational (left brain) side that also speaks. Most business organizations do not hire musicians, poets, or artists who have learned to restrain their analytical side to provide a front row seat for their ingenious side. This means providers must convince a customer there is safety and well-being outside their imagination's cocoon. Providers must become imagination pathfinders, promoting bravery to the customer's timid imagination. This secret will explore ways to play that pathfinder role through how you demonstrate you are worthy of trust.

Trust is a core feature of all innovation cultures since it serves as an antidote to the judgmental close inspection that can retard ideas. Co-creation partnerships, as anxiety-free alliances, are all about paying attention to the trust gap, that emotional space between expectation and fulfillment and between hope and evidence. All customer relationships begin with a promise made or implied: "We'll be landing on time," "It will be ready by noon," or "Your order will be right out." Granted, great service recovery can transform an aggrieved customer into a mollified one. But the residue of betrayal will leave a disappointed customer perpetually on guard for the time when letdown reoccurs.

Trust means a readiness to take risks with your customer. It is a willingness to go forward with hope without looking back with apprehension. The foundation of that disposition requires opening up with sensitive information, feelings, or views with the expectation your partner will feel encouraged to do likewise. It is not a drive-by process but rather one that requires time and patience.

Goldcorp, a Canadian company that finds, extracts, and processes gold, had a mine called Red Lake in northwestern Ontario. It was not producing the amount of gold expected, plus the gold market was depressed. CEO Rob McEwen was attending a seminar on Linux, an open-source operating system. "Why not create open-source mining?" He created the Goldcorp Challenge—anyone who could tell Goldcorp where to mine would get prizes worth up to $100,000. But here is the trust part. He did something no one had ever done. He turned over all their super-secret data on the Red Lake mine online. Over fourteen hundred geologists from fifty countries participated in the challenge. The winner was a company from West Perth, Australia. When Goldcorp drilled the sites the winner had predicted from their modeling, Goldcorp hit on all four. Today Goldcorp is the world's fourth-largest producer of gold.[1]

Trust is honor in action, the soul of a partnership covenant. A covenant is more vow than pact. It is undergirded by a moral pledge, not just a contractual one. We rely on it to govern fair and proper practice. Customer interactions aren't generally regulated by formal contracts that bind provider and customer to virtuous behaviors—customers simply assume they will be treated in a respectful, ethical, and civil manner.

Trust has three components in the context of co-creation partnerships (figure 6). It first begins with the whole truth. "If you want to be trusted, be honest," goes the old saying. "If you want to be honest, be true. If you want to be true, be yourself." Authentic candor and squeaky-clean dealings telegraph a purity that communicates to your customer's imagination that it is safe to come out. It emboldens your customer's imagination to tell the customer's logic to be quiet and wait its turn.

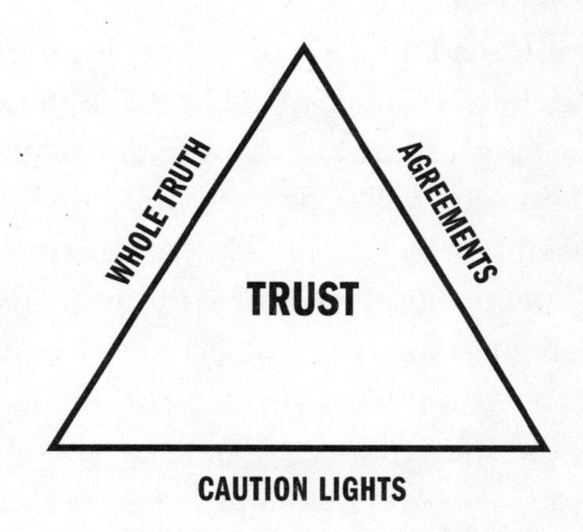

FIGURE 6. The elements of partnership trust

Second, trust relies on work agreements that reflect mutual expectations. These are the establishment and communication of what each promises the other. Keeping promises requires knowing the guarantees made. Smart promise keepers also recognize the players in the partnership are imperfect people. Misunderstandings, mistakes, and miscalculations can plague any relationship and put it at risk of being derailed. Wisdom comes in making "caution lights for covenants" a part of the partnership expectations. Partners feel secure if there is already a partnership preventive-maintenance plan in place.

Customers don't expect providers to be perfect; they do expect them to care. And in the case of co-creation partnerships, they expect them to care deeply about the welfare of their partner as well as the wellness of their relationship. Renovating a broken relationship after a partnership glitch can return the union to productivity, often with a bond stronger than before.

All my life I thought leaves departed trees in the fall because they got too old to hang onto the branch and gravity bested their grasp. It does not work that way. Trees literally release their leaves from the limb. It made me think about a customer releasing their imagination to be used in the resolution of a problem or challenge. Here is how a leaf becomes the prey of gravity. As days get colder and shorter, trees create a hormone that sends out a chemical message and triggers the creation of cells that appear at the spot where the leaf stem meets the branch. These abscission (root word for scissors) cells make a microscopic-sized cut that gradually severs the leaf from the branch. Trust is like a leaf's chemical message to your customer's imagination. It changes the imagination's holding onto the safety of the bedroom of familiarity so the imagination willingly falls onto the playground of innovation.

CHAPTER 10

Start Partnering with the Whole Truth

The truth is funny. Honest discovery, observation, and reaction is better than contrived invention.

—DEL CLOSE

"What is the main cause of partnership failure?" It was a question I posed to my lunch partner, Dr. Carl Rogers, in the early eighties. I had just finished reading his book *A Way of Being*.[1] "Trouble with the truth," he told me. I probed a bit further: "You mean people lie to each other?" He continued, "That is not quite what I mean. It is not the lies, it's the deception. They have trouble with the *whole* truth. And once that wholeness goes, they have to work very hard to get it back. Some people just don't want to work that hard."

His words are especially fitting in our present-day era of acceptability of half-truths. Co-creation partnerships require the "whole and nothing but" kind of truth. It is the main ingredient of trust, a major culprit in its demise, and a part of the remedy in its return once lost. It is more than compassionate candor; it is deeper than authenticity; it is revealing your soul in a way that purifies connections. It is goodness personified.

Before we proceed, let's recap. Your customers' imagination is needed to help you solve their problem or fulfil their need or aspiration. A co-creation partnership with them not only enhances their loyalty, it enriches the quality of the result. Trust is a necessary feature to foster a milieu of security. When you say, "I trust that person," consider what enables you to operate with her or him in an unguarded fashion. One of the central components of trust is a history of promise-keeping. We hear it in lines like "her word is her bond" or "what he says you can take to the bank." Truth-telling is so sacred we sometimes put words like "gospel" in front of it.

Ever wonder why electricians refer to an ineffective electrical connection as a "bad" connection, as if it were misbehaving? A good connection electrically is one that has grounding, one without interference in its flow of energy, and one that delivers all the power it is capable of delivering. That is a perfect description for the role that truth plays in a partnership—grounded, ideal flow of energy, and full power. But we live in a time of "bad connections" and must take extra steps to counter their spin and distortion of the truth.

Tell the Truth, the Whole Truth, and Nothing But . . .

"Ladies and gentlemen, another on-time arrival by Mayday Airlines," the pilot announced as my plane pulled up to the jetway. A quick look at my always-accurate smartphone revealed we were actually fourteen minutes past the posted time I had told my client the flight was scheduled to arrive. I later learned that "on time" in the commercial-flight arrival world had a fifteen-minute grace period. A pilot once told me it was like EBIT (earnings before interest and taxes). "The FAA built in a fudge factor for 'on time' since we cannot control the airfield traffic while we are taxiing to the gate any more than your employees can impact interest and taxes."

But what about customer transparency? What about the promise made or implied to passengers? Can you imagine the lyrics of Lerner and Loewe's *My Fair Lady* tune being changed to "Get me to the church within fifteen minutes of the wedding time"? Or how T-minus countdowns might impact rocket launches if there were a fudge (a.k.a. fib) factor? If on time truly meant "on time," would there not be a greater incentive for airlines to collectively demand greater efficiency on the airfield and tarmac, since they all would be getting dinged for unavailable gates or tardy ground crews?

Let's take another common experience with the acceptability of half-truths—the drive-thru window at any quick service restaurant. Last week I stopped midmorning at one and ordered a breakfast to go. There was no one behind me in the drive-thru lane. The very nice person asked if I would pull across the lot and park; someone would bring out my order to me. It has happened many times. "Why don't I just stay here," I suggested to her. "When my order is ready, you won't have to have someone take the time to bring it all the way across the parking lot, you can just hand it to me right here. I promise to move to the parking lot if another vehicle comes up behind me."

"Oh, no," she said. "You will have to move your car now because if you sit here, you will mess up my numbers for wait time in the drive-thru." I gave this confusing issue one more attempt. "But won't that give your restaurant a false read? If you keep faking the actual wait time by sending me away, what incentive will there be to speed up the operation inside that caused my trip to the 'wait lot' in the first place?" She could not deal with this cognitive dissonance and pleaded, "Please don't get me in trouble with my manager." A completely inefficient procedure predicated on maintaining a bald-faced lie solely for the sake of important, but deceptive, metrics!

So, how does this fit in with gaining access to your customer's imagination? Lockheed Martin was in a dead-heat race with Boeing to win a $200 billion contract to build the F-35 Joint Strike fighter plane. It would be the largest contract ever awarded a private company by the federal government. Early indications were that the decision makers at the Pentagon favored the Boeing prototype. I was a consultant to Lockheed's Lean Sigma LM21 team under the leadership of Mike Joyce. He put it this way: "We did two important things. We found ways to get inside our customers' heads by being relentlessly inquisitive. We staged countless focus groups with contractors, customers, and pilots to unearth their blunt honesty on 'the good, the bad, and the ugly.'" An innovation turning point came when it was learned from fighter fliers that the aesthetics of the aircraft, not just the aeronautics, were very important. Their message was, "Don't put me in the cockpit of an ugly aircraft." Lockheed won with a much more attractive fighter plane.[2]

Make Honesty a Best Practice, Not a Best Policy

The Delta regional jet was packed. As the flight backed away from the gate, the flight attendant began her ritualistic safety spiel about seatbelts, sudden turbulence, and smoking. She ended by saying, "The flying time to Grand Rapids will be two hours . . . no, it will be an hour and a half . . . no, actually, I don't know." The cabin erupted with laughter and applause. What jolted the half-asleep plane-full into cheering? Unscripted, unadulterated raw honesty! We loved her total candor and confident authenticity. But we loved even more her purity of intent and demonstration of innocence!

> **Truth-telling takes enough compassion to send the very best; truth-hearing takes enough humility to receive the very worst.**

We grow up hearing "honesty is the best policy." As adults we hear half-truths portrayed as honesty. Politicians keep secret the number of paramilitary civilians fighting in a troubled spot to disguise the true size of the military engagement—a number the public would not tolerate. The super-low price loudly advertised comes with fine print describing a rebate only claimed by sending in a pound of paperwork. And when we hear the radio ad end with a super-fast-talking guy rattling off all the exceptions and disclaimers, we know we are not hearing raw honesty.

Honesty shortens the distance between people. It frees partners from the anxiety and caution involved in having to remember what they made up when they strayed from the truth. It triggers a connection with the humanity in each of us. And in that space, we are quicker to forgive, more tolerant of error, and much more accepting of "Actually, I don't know." Honesty is not a "best policy"; honesty is a "best practice."

Ultimate Software provides cloud-based human-capital-management software and has won numerous awards for extraordinary customer service. *Fortune* ranked them number

8 in 2019 on their "Best Places to Work For" list. *Forbes* ranked them number 7 on their "Most Innovative Growth Companies" list. The company is also famous for including customers, encouraged to be boldly honest, in the design and enhancements of their software programs. Here is an example.

A retail customer needed employee-performance-feedback functionality within their Ultimate software that would ensure anonymity for the feedback provider. The retailer participated with Ultimate in iterative design review, providing insights, specific requirements, and design suggestions along the way. Ultimate's product/design team asked specific questions about the need for thresholds on the number of responses to ensure the feedback was anonymous, when and how such thresholds should be applied, and how flexible those choices should be. The result was a collaboratively designed feature/capability that was released into the product early in 2019 during the product's beta cycle.

Never Tell Your Partner a White Lie

When witnesses take the stand in a trial and place their right hand on the Bible, they are required to swear to "tell the truth, the whole truth, and nothing but the truth." Why not just promise to "tell the truth"? A full three-truths oath is crafted to prevent the telling of "white lies." White lies are defined as "a polite or harmless lie" and are contrasted with "black lies"—those with evil or malicious intent. But are the white ones really polite or harmless? Izey Odiase wrote, "Don't lie to protect my feelings. I'd rather you speak the truth with love and respect. I'll be fine!"

We use white lies when we compliment someone ("Your cake was delicious" or "That is an attractive dress") even though our spoken words differ from our true belief. We tell a prospect we are pitching that the item she desires should arrive in two days even when we know four days is the most likely delivery time. We communicate to a vendor, "The check is in the mail," and then quickly back up our "white lie" to make reality catch up with our falsehood.

White lies are unadulterated deception, regardless of their "benevolent" intent. They help us save face but do little to promote a solid partnership. We use them in awkward moments when we believe we lack sufficient time to craft an honest but unhurtful response. We view white lies as a governor on bluntness. As such, we rely on them as a form of interpersonal cowardice. Their presence in fair-weather relationships might be accepted by most as diplomacy, but in partnerships they are unmistakably deceptive.

A group of operations leaders with the Freeman Company, a large convention-services and exhibit-management company, was working on how to partner more effectively with convention-center operations people who unloaded trucks and got exhibitors' display material to their booths before the start of a convention. An example of a "runaround promise" came up. This is a scenario in which you haven't quite completed a customer's request at the time they inquire about it, but you state it is done (when it actually is a work in progress) and then run around quickly to make your white lie the truth. "Hell, no!" said Keith Kennedy, the head of operations at the time. "Let's always be completely honest no matter if a lie is right on the edge of being true. It is about our character, not our bottom line."

Would you trust Keith? Genuine and bold assertions in the face of marginal truths send unmistakable signals to your customer's imagination that it has a safe harbor to visit the customer's challenge, need, or aspiration. After Keith retired, Freeman created the Keith Kennedy Service Quality Award, given each year to the employee who demonstrated a "true blue" attitude in delivering over-the-top service to customers.

"I'm not upset that you lied to me," wrote philosopher Friedrich Nietzsche, "I'm upset that from now on I can't believe you." Truth-telling frees customers from anxiety and caution. It triggers a strong bond of faith with another. And in that connection, we are quicker to forgive, more tolerant of error, and much more accepting of "Honestly, I don't know." Tell your co-creation partners the truth, the whole truth, no holds barred. While acquiring a few Pinocchio's noses might seem a tame imperfection, their very presence is like a cancer that if allowed to grow can become fatal to your partnership.

Start Partnering with the Whole Truth: The Partnering Crib Notes

Be open with your customer in the discussion of truth-telling. Outline "what ifs" that provide partnership preparation for failures to be truthful. Remember, everything in your customer's experience is personal. Become known as someone who "always does what you say you will do." Avoid corporate speak and sanitized legalese communications. They can, by definition, violate the whole truth principle. It is practices—values in action—that your customers care about. They do not care about your policies, procedures, or authorities. Instead of dwelling on why "we can't," focus on finding a path to "yes, we can!" Truthful service is that laced with the unmistakable pursuit of honesty on both sides of the alliance.

No relationship is likely to be perfect all the time. The healthy customer partnership, like a healthy marriage, is marked by candor and welcomed critique. Honesty fuels more honesty if defensiveness is absent. And as candor triggers improvement, those who serve feel responsive, those served feel heard and valued, and the partnership feels healthy. In the words of Marcellinus, "The language of truth is unadorned and always simple."

When you stretch the truth, watch out for the snapback.

—BILL COPELAND

CHAPTER 11

Set Innovation Working Agreements

Nobody rises to low expectations.

—CALVIN LLOYD

My three granddaughters are reaching the age when driving is a really big deal. My oldest just got her driver's license; the middle one is not far behind. And all three want to log happy time behind the steering wheel of their parents' golf cart at the beach. It means they are now old enough to start noticing the "customs of driving." Not the rules, mind you, the implied agreements and expectations drivers have with and of each other.

We were at a stoplight, and I was planning to turn left after the light changed. I waited for the oncoming car on the other side of the light to pass before turning left. My youngest granddaughter, Cassie, asked, "How did you know to wait? You got to the traffic light before he did." I explained there was an agreement that you never turn left into oncoming traffic. Shortly after that, we came to a four-way stop with no light involved. I waited my turn based on who had arrived first at the stop sign. "More agreements, right?" she asked.

Establishing and updating work agreements is the business end of a co-creation partnership. In some ways, work agreements provide the foundation for justice in the relationship. Skipping over this part can put the partnership at peril since you risk leaving it open to misunderstanding, confusion, and even error. Agreements are the spoken-out-loud reflection of expectations, and they help ensure the partnership operates with maximum productivity. When a merchant agrees to deliver a product by a set hour, it creates an expectation in the recipient that might be the basis of all types of their plans. Failing to keep that agreement not only creates disappointment and erodes reliability, it destroys the productivity of the recipient. It is a betrayal, a breach of faith, and a violation of partnership justice.

In Secret 2: Grounding, we focused on the importance of value-based guardrails. So it might seem we are covering the same ground here. But there is a difference. Guardrails guide the soul of the relationship; expectations (manifested as work agreements) guide the work of the relationship. Guardrails make the relationship effective; work agreements make it efficient. Guardrails say "let's be totally honest"; work agreements say "let's get this done by Thursday." Both are needed to lend trust to the alliance.

Work agreements can sound like strict rules: all emails must be answered within twenty-four hours. The best ones sound far more interesting and serve as memorable guidelines. San Antonio-based Touchstone Communities uses agreements like "Honor time: if you are not early, you are late" and "Err on the side of inclusion—if you are in doubt, ask too many rather than not enough." The language is as memorable as it is instructional, yet the line between compliance and infraction is clear. When I was in army basic training, the agreement was, "If it moves, salute it; if it doesn't, pick it up; if you can't pick it up, paint it." The sentiment contained in the agreement was unmistakable. This chapter will focus on perspectives to guide the crafting and managing of partnership work agreements.

Write Work Agreements with "Visible Ink"

The ad was on the back page of a Superman comic book—a pen that would write in invisible ink. For a while I thought I was Superman, and I had the shirt with a giant "S" to prove it. I saved up chores money and ordered the amazing, magical pen. I had my sister write on a piece of paper a secret word in the invisible ink with my magic pen. Since I was Superman, I would be able to tell her what she had written. After she wrote the word, I privately took the paper into the living room, turned on the lamp, and voila! I could read her secret note. She was impressed! That is, until she figured out she could do the same thing with lemon juice and a Q-tip. And her "magic pen" was free! The invisible-ink pen quickly lost its charm.

Agreements must never be in "invisible ink." They must be public, prominent, and perpetual. They must be known by all who will be influenced by them. They must be positioned where they can be easily seen and remembered. You know the agreements are working as guidelines when someone simply points at them to rein in violations that endanger interpersonal efficiency or inhibit progress. Finally, they must be perpetual. Never let the shiny wear off of work agreements.

My wife and I had someone tape our wedding ceremony. At that time, the only media for recording was a Sears, Roebuck reel-to-reel tape recorder. It was later converted to a 33⅓ rpm record, then a cassette tape, and then a DVD, and finally put on a flash drive. Every anniversary we play it as a reminder of the agreements made at the church altar in front of friends and family. "Renewing your partnership vows" can keep the relationship fresh, maintain top-of-mind guidance, and ensure discipline and trustworthiness.

Make Partnership Agreements Inclusive

Co-creation partnerships have agreements that are collectively crafted, not borrowed from another occasion or group, nor copied from a textbook. The process of harmonizing on agreements is what makes them work. They are made by hand, so to speak, not store bought or borrowed from a neighbor. And in the process of their creation, there is opportunity for a meeting of the minds and a joining of the spirits.

Gloria Steinem was a rock star of feminism in 1985. The editor of *Ms.* magazine, she reigned as the supreme spokesperson for all things related to the movement. And I saw her standing in the middle of the giant print room of Quad/Graphics, a high-end printing company headquartered in Sussex, Wisconsin. Quad printed her magazine. I was there to teach at the Quad/University, a three-day event where the entire company was turned over to the frontline employees so every supervisor could go through training classes. I got a tour the day before the training.

"She visits here a lot," an employee told me on my tour, as I watched from the second floor. Gloria was holding court with several press operators in front of a giant printing press. "And they really listen to her ideas. In fact, apparently there was an agreement she and Harry Quadracci (the founder and CEO at the time) made that he could comment on her magazine content if she could comment on his printing plant operation." It worked. Gloria was invited to start the presses at their Lomira plant's grand opening.

Two points were important in this example. Harry Quadracci wanted more than a typical provider-customer relationship; to paraphrase a song from *The Music Man*, he wanted a partnership with a capital P that rhymes with C that stands for creativity. Second, they established work agreements that leveraged mutuality and clarified boundaries. Gloria was "on the floor" in the full sense of the phrase. Such clarity of expectations laced with trust created a freedom much like giving a neighbor a spare key to your house.

Plan Clear Feedback Cues

Cues are interpersonal signals that help keep partners on track and in sync with their agreements. Smart partnerships treasure early warnings, of course, but they do expect surprises. To deal with these surprises, they agree in advance on cues—signals or agreements that ensure their interpersonal connections continue harmoniously. Think of them like your significant other kicking you under the table at a dinner party when you are talking too loudly, or publicly telling something you should keep private.

My wife has a unique way of delivering a cue. When I am on the road for several days and come home late on Friday in a bit of a dark mood, she softly says, "I can see you've been to the hateful school!" (Translation: keep that attitude up, big boy, and you'll likely miss out on some social activities you were counting on this weekend!) She'd be kicking me under the table about now!

Cues are a shorthand way to give feedback so that your partner can adjust the performance. However, sometimes cues need to be elevated to more than a nonverbal gesture or a code word. Your partner requires more direct feedback. A partnership must be based on living agreements and always evolving to accommodate changing conditions and unforeseen circumstances. There are three steps that can make feedback powerful and fruitful, from my book *Managers as Mentors: Building Partnerships for Learning*.

STEP 1: CREATE A CLIMATE OF IDENTIFICATION.

Your first objective as a provider is to enhance receptivity by showing that you identify with your partner. Start with comments that have an "I am like you"—that is, "not perfect"—kind of message. Telegraph your empathy, respect, and admiration. Partners can hear even the strongest feedback if it is delivered with concern and compassion. This need not be a major production—just a sentence or two to establish rapport.

STEP 2: STATE THE RATIONALE FOR THE FEEDBACK.

Effective feedback is given in context, not out of the blue. When you hear feedback and end up thinking, "Where did that come from?" or "Why are you telling me this?" you have probably been given feedback without context. The issue is not subtlety or diplomacy, it is understanding. Help your partner gain a clear sense of why the feedback is being given.

STEP 3: ASSUME YOU'RE GIVING YOURSELF THE FEEDBACK.

Besides being clear and empathetic, feedback must be straightforward and honest. This does not mean it must be blunt or cruel; it means that your partner should not be left wondering, "What did she *not* tell me that I needed to hear?" Trust is born of clean communication. Think of your goal this way: How would you deliver the feedback if you were giving it to yourself? Think about your own preferences; give feedback as you would wish to receive it. Always check for understanding to make certain your partner heard what you intended.[1]

Put a Banjo in Your Partnership Orchestra

Béla Fleck is arguably the greatest banjo player in the world. He is the winner of sixteen Grammy Awards, and his amazing repertoire ranges from bluegrass to classical. He made news in the music world when he wrote a banjo concerto called *The Imposter* and performed it with symphony orchestras around the country to sold-out crowds.

> Agreements are statements of promise, the blueprints of cooperation.
> They promote a meeting of the minds, the deterrent to disappointment.

A banjo in a symphony? Banjos don't go with Bach and Beethoven. They belong with square dances, pizza parlors, and having-a-great-time gatherings. Symphonies are supposed to be serious highbrow sounds appreciated by intellectuals who wear tuxedos and gowns and drink Manhattans. Banjos go with blue jeans and people who prefer a cold beer. But think of a banjo as a metaphor for adding playfulness to your work pacts.

You started life as a banjo! Early in your life you giggled, took few things seriously, and assertively leaped into silly games with the single goal of having fun, not winning. You were as innately fair and kind to kids around you as you were to the stuffed toy you cherished. As you entered socialization school and the success institute, you realized the banjo was not a serious instrument for work life. At first your transformation was uncomfortable and awkward. Later you forgot ever being a banjo and worked as an "imposter." Oh, you got a glimpse of the banjo when you played with your kids. But such folly was left in the workplace parking lot.

Well, guess what? Innovation dances to the sweet sound of a banjo. Banjo behavior makes people want to jump up and join in. It changes melancholy to magical and reserved to sociable. Banjo joy helps foster in customers the rhythmical tapping of happy feet, not the intolerant drumming of impatient fingers. Use banjo thinking to guide your agreement setting. Too much somberness is the antithesis of imagination. Wake up your funny bone, wear a zany hat to every meeting, and add a fun touch to your work agreements. Spice up your collective expectations with a bit of whimsy and weirdness; it goes with the territory. "You can't leave the meeting if someone else's beeper goes off," "If one person gets to go to the bathroom, we all do," "Nobody gets hurt today," or my favorite, "Start every meeting with a joke."

Innovate means to "make new." And that means boldly abandoning what is "not new." It means rewriting the status quo and breaking with the norm. It means challenging the rules. Breaking the rules is not an invitation for mutinous behavior or defiant militancy. It is an invitation to bravely be unique and daringly pioneer an ingenious approach with your customer. Pablo Picasso wrote, "Learn the rules like a pro so you can break them like an artist." Value discipline by making your work agreements the foundation for accountability, not a boon to mindless participation that can rob the relationship of soul, spirit, and sensitivity. "Just following the rules" can be the father of mediocrity and the mother of ordinary.

Set Innovation Working Agreements: The Partnering Crib Notes

Take time in every initial innovation meeting to craft clear expectations. Make them fun, make them tough, and make them tailored to fit the goals of your alliance, the values you want to spotlight, and the personalities of the players. Keep them public so they are constant reminders. Craft them in such a fashion that partners will feel compelled to respect, bound to apply, and committed to defend them. Keep them adaptable to fit the inevitable changes likely to impact and potentially disrupt your relationship. Ensure they are (and feel) inclusive and collaborative so each person impacted by them can comfortably shape their origin and influence their evolution. Remember, clear agreements without crisp execution are only good intentions. In the end, all the planning and goal setting is just "getting ready to." Execution is the true test of commitment. "I believe, I support, I approve" are weasel words unless they are coupled with visible demonstration.

Expectations are more than road signs along the journey to a goal, they are lessons in partnership decorum. Like the "politeness" norms you heard repeated by your parents as you grew up, they teach co-creation partners how to act "civilized" in an arena of chaotic creation. They serve as a mentor that helps sponsor wild imagination by controlling its excesses without caging its gifts. As such, they enable warnings to play nicely with wacky.

It takes real planning to organize this kind of chaos.

—MEL ODOM

CHAPTER 12

Heed Caution Lights for Contracts

The time to repair the roof is when the sun is shining.

—JOHN F. KENNEDY

Tim Love beat the Iron Chef! And right after that TV competition episode, I partnered with him to prepare a dinner for eight. But let me unpack this story a bit slower.

Tim Love is a renowned chef and the owner of a number of restaurants in Tennessee and Texas, including the elegant Southwestern-themed Lonesome Dove Bistro in the famous Fort Worth Stockyards. When he is not preparing Rocky Mountain elk ribeye or wild boar, he is on TV, especially cooking shows like Food Network's *Best in Smoke*, CNBC's *Restaurant Startup*, and Bravo TV's *Top Chef Masters*. You may have seen him on NBC's *The Today Show* and ABC's *Good Morning America*. I knew Tim from the time I lived in Dallas and would enjoy a burger at his Love Shack restaurant.

One of my clients rented a home near the Augusta National Golf Club for the week of the Masters golf tournament and invited me, along with six other friends, to come for dinner one evening. He also flew in Tim Love from Dallas to cook for us. Since I live only an hour away from the famous golf course,

Tim asked if I would stop by a grocery store to pick up a few items he did not bring on his flight—portabella mushrooms, whole garlic, and asparagus.

We did not watch Chef Love cook. Our gourmet steak dinner was a collective creation. And Tim tried a few twists to the dinner he claimed he had never used before. Plus, he gave us cooking lessons in the process. One I will always remember was his "prepare for the preparation" wisdom. "Think through in detail what might go wrong and how you will react," he told us. Parchment paper cuts clean-up time in half. Put a waste bucket near the cutting board. Place the most frequently used cooking tools nearby. And always have an extra pair of kitchen shears on hand.

It was a grand meal. But even grander was creating the meal with a master chef, knowing we were all prepared for what would happen . . . and for what might have happened. It exemplified the way of a co-creation partnership at its best.

Prevent What Might Have Been

"For all sad words of tongue and pen," lamented John Greenleaf Whittier, "the saddest are these, 'it might have been.'" Countless partnerships look back with regret that they encountered a hiccup, were unprepared for how to effectively deal with it, and experienced a promising relationship completely derail. Looking back, many have mourned just like Whittier. But setbacks can be different if you "prepare for the preparation." Love's advice is analogous to the carpentry adage "measure twice and cut once."

Contingency plans are the staple of firefighters, emergency rooms, and smart businesses. They are the "what if" scripts that guide rehearsals, dry runs, fire drills, and a host of preparedness scenarios. They enable those impacted to proceed, as my partner John Patterson advises, with the three Cs: calm, competence, and confidence. They are the antidotes to spur-of-the-moment improvisations that can falter or fail under the weight of poor discipline. They are symbolically the orange caution lights that warn us that a red-light danger zone is just ahead.

Relationship planning can be a boon to weathering a sudden storm without getting soaked. Building into the relationship warning signs and agreed-upon expectations and practices related to the predictable type of "what ifs" gives the partnership a sense of security. It provides the comfort that says, "We thought this might happen and at calmer times we talked through precisely what we would do if it did."

Watch Out for the Danger Zones

Disruption in a partnership generally does not begin with noisy conflict or the fire of an interpersonal skirmish; it is smokier than that. It can be triggered by a half-truth, a small broken promise, a self-centered perspective, or simply indifference. It can come from outside the relationship in the form of a reorganization, shifting leadership priorities, or changes in a competitive strategy. It is a "pinch" in the tie that binds. At a minimum, it leads partners to question the depth of their commitment to the relationship. Left unchecked, an aggrieved partner shifts from solid partnership loyalty to the "zone of indifference."

The zone of indifference is characterized by a sense of uncertainty. With emotional allegiance vulnerable, a partner (or partners) begins to consider options for resolution and/or routes to remedy the emotional dissonance, sometimes including an exit strategy. But the zone of indifference carries another feature beyond a yellow-light pinch. It sets up the partnership for a dark tipping point, the spark that ignites exit.

When a pharmaceutical company and a vendor severed their ties on the verge of a breakthrough, the vendor claimed it was because he was late for a meeting. The pharmaceutical company representative described a series of broken promises that had been festering for a long time—late for one meeting was simply the final straw, the tipping point. Avoiding such a rupture takes early attentiveness and bold assertiveness. That all can be made easier if anticipated through preparation.

A meeting was held between the leadership of a privately held audio sound company and the leadership of a large vendor. They had had major conflicts over an extended period of time. Under normal circumstances, they would have "divorced." But the vendor had a unique offering that the audio sound company needed, and the audio sound company was a very large customer to the vendor. Early in the meeting the facilitator had the two leadership groups work in separate rooms to write on a flip chart two lists: "Stupid Things We Think They Do" and "Stupid Things They Think We Do." When the charts were revealed and compared, it triggered a healthy conversation about myths, erroneous beliefs, and unfounded rumors that had long plagued their relationship.

The "pinch," a label coined by professors John Sherwood and Jack Glidewell, led to a discussion that the audio company labeled "Locker Room Talk."[1] The image of what happens during halftime in a football game came from the company's CEO, who is a major fan of the Miami Dolphins. He "thinks in football" and uses words that are football terms—goal line, scoreboard, defensive coach, tailback, you name it. The Locker Room Talk between the audio company's and vendor's leadership created new agreements and a decision to have more "halftime" pinch discussions. The relationship continues to flourish as the audio sound company has tripled in size.

Pinches are the front edge of "something is not quite right here." Your intuition signals that some feature or fact makes the partnership feel out of balance. If it were a medical condition, it would be comparable to a sore throat—not the malady, just the early warning of the malady. And it warrants immediate attention, clarity, and most of all, courage. Care enough to raise a warning flag. Even if your gut is wrong, it signals to your partner you care about the relationship and want to keep it healthy.

Clear Away Partnership Booby Traps

How do we plan for preparation? Start by surfacing potential partnership booby traps. A booby trap is something embedded in the players or the relationship that could lead to a source of conflict. It involves more than simply sharing expectations for the partnership, it includes revealing aspects about yourself that might be beneficial for the other partner to know. When I facilitate innovation sessions with clients and their customers, I ask each to disclose to the other answers to these three questions and a statement:

- What are ways I typically help a partnership?
- What are ways I typically hinder a partnership?
- What are my concerns about being a part of this one?
- You can help me not screw this one up by . . .

Often the roles in a partnership between a provider and a customer are quite clear. However, there are formal roles and then there are informal roles. Who will lead the discussion? Who will be responsible for note-taking, record keeping, scheduling, and retaining documents (like flip chart sheets) to be used again in a future meeting? Is there a time-keeper role? What about decision rights? What about inviting guests? What about including a substitute if a key person must be absent? Lack of discussion of issues like these can result in a booby trap down the road.

Discuss the Disruption

Disruption is inevitable; only the length of time disruption lingers varies. It leaves the partnership unstable and less productive because of its unsettling force. Start with exploring all the likely "what ifs" that could plague the relationship down the road along with crafting a strategy for how you plan to deal with it. The Ten Questions for Partnership Preparation can become a part of the "prepare for the preparation."

TEN QUESTIONS FOR PARTNERSHIP PREPARATION

1. How do I typically react to an interpersonal-conflict situation?
2. How will our partnership be impacted if one of us has to take a break for a while?
3. What happens if one of us cannot continue, yet the partnership needs to continue?
4. If things go wrong, are our early warning and repair skills compatible?

5. If one of us is adversely affected strategically by this partnership, are there ways to support that partner?
6. Are there cultural or marketplace changes down the road that could damage our partnership?
7. Have we agreed on the consequences of delays or missed deadlines?
8. Are our respective organizations structured to support this partnership?
9. Do privacy and confidentiality mean the same to each of us?
10. Do we agree on how to allocate the returns, profits, or benefits from this partnership?

Stop Partnership Pain before Getting Injured

Pain. At some point it enters the backdoor of every partnership of any duration. Sometimes, it announces its presence loudly and with a fit of frenzy. Other times, it quietly sneaks in like smoke slowly filling the room of relationship until its authority demands attention. It can be an irritant to be dealt with and dismissed. It can be a handicap that keeps the liaison wounded. And it can be like a code blue, sounding a warning of demise.

How do you spot the front edge of subtle partnership pain? First, look inward. Reflect on the current state of the partnership. What emotion surfaces as your mind skims across the then-until-now history of your partnership? Focus on your feelings. Do you feel guilty? Partnership guilt feels like a hollowness in your gut and a dread in your heart, like when you are out of town on a red-letter day of a significant relationship and forget to call. Do you have a sense of indebtedness? Do you hope meetings with your partner will stay superficial and not get too deep?

Now, look outward. Has your partnership communication become tired, wooden, without a totally authentic feeling? Does your dialogue sound a bit robotic? Is there a bit of dread when thinking about the next encounter? Do you sense something is being hidden from you? Is your partner micromanaging you in a fashion more extreme than when you began? Do you feel there is emotional distance? If there were a rheostat on your partnership, would it be shining dim? All these could be signs of partnership pain. Now what?

Partnership pain can be a natural part of growth, a path to distinction, or it can signal rocky times ahead. Pain is a "yellow light" warning; injury is a "red light," danger-ahead warning. When I was in army jungle survival school in Panama, the master sergeant separated physical discomfort into two categories: pain and injury. "If you are in pain, suck it up and learn from it," he told us. "However, if you are injured, let us know and we will get you a medic. We do not want you injured."

The feature that makes co-creation partnerships more vulnerable to pain than most regular partnerships or relationships is their freewheeling side of imagination-in-action. According to neuroscientist Nancy Andreasen, author of *The Creative Brain*, the creative person "may have to confront criticism or rejection for being too questioning or too unconventional. Too much openness means living on the edge. Sometimes the person may drop over the edge . . ."[2]

Be willing to call a time out. It sounds like, "I could be wrong, but I am sensing our partnership is not working as we had hoped it would. What are your thoughts?" This can trigger a discussion on what's working and what is not. Sometimes a structured approach makes an awkward discussion less so. The Partnership Checkup tool at the end of this book can be a guide to your conversation. It provides a reflection part and a discussion-guide part. While this tool is particularly helpful when there is relationship tension, it can also be useful as preventive maintenance. You take your car and your body in for a periodic checkup, why not an important partnership?

Plan Caution Lights for Contracts

Planned renegotiation uses the incident of the pinch to discuss likely scenarios of partnership disruption down the road and explores how the partnership would potentially deal with these incidents. Since this book focuses on innovation, I have included a song I wrote titled "Caution Lights for Contracts" (figure 7). The lyrics of the song tell the tale—the goal is no fault self-esteem. How do we approach conflicts and disruptions in a fashion that does not blame or render guilt? It makes smooth a road to success that might otherwise be rocky.

Now, let's go one step further. When firefighters respond to a fire, their actions reflect pit crew precision. They did not acquire this level of performance excellence by sitting at the chow table at the fire station and talking through their actions. They drilled through dry runs and performance rehearsal. It is the same with great partnerships. Don't be afraid to practice saying words that soothe in times of discord, clarify in moments of confusion, and diplomatically confront in instances when chutzpa is most needed. It helps a plan become more of an instruction manual.

FIGURE 7. Caution lights for contracts

Heed Caution Lights for Contracts: The Partnering Crib Notes

Be thorough in how you "prepare for preparation" by surfacing potential booby traps and together exploring tactics to defuse them. Respect the plural version of self-esteem; that is, hold your relationship in high regard by bolstering collective confidence. Be attentive to any sense that things are not quite right within the partnership. Be bold in saying what you feel and seeking maximum candor in the partnership. Recognize that partnerships are not iron-clad relationships; they work best when they are flexible. Adaptability, like life, is the key to survival (with a hat tip to Charlie Darwin). Don't Band-Aid conflicts; build in the agreements that keep them from reoccurring. Effective partnerships, especially co-creation partnerships, depend on discipline. Always make time immediately for partnership discussions and build into your schedule regular meeting time to discuss how the partnership is working.

"Planning is bringing the future into the present so that you can do something about it now," wrote time management guru Alan Lakein. That means examining as many of the "what ifs" as you can with full recognition that there will always be twists and turns as well as highs and lows on your journey to success. Partnership glitches can be a friendly tutor only if you heed their early warnings, use them as a diagnostic tool, and always think of them as an important resource for partner and partnership growth. Respect pain—but never make pain your friend. Partners who welcome pain as their friend soon find it staying for supper. And when it has overstayed its welcome, pain catches you not looking and eats all the dessert.

A Look Ahead: Passion

People with passion can make their impossible dreams come true. Passion fuels high-wattage innovation. It is as infectious as a grin, as inspirational as a newborn, and as inviting as a crackling fire and a cup of hot cider on a cold, wintry evening. It has a permanent seat at the table of invention, one crafted through centuries of favor from all seeking opportunity, adventure, and growth. In our fifth and final secret, we will unfold the majesty and magic of passion. The section will come in several forms—a portrait, a plan, and a set of instructions for practical application. If the pursuit of customer imagination were a religion, passion would be its hymnal.

If we manage conflict constructively, we harness its energy for creativity and development.

—KENNETH KAYE

Secret 5

PASSION

Never Stop Courting

Purpose is the reason you journey.
Passion is the fire that lights your way.

—ANONYMOUS

Ten years ago, when my wife and I celebrated our fortieth wedding anniversary, someone at the celebration gathering asked my wife, "How have you and Chip stayed happily married all these many years?" I was expecting a funny comment about it being easy since I was on the road all the time. But she got serious. "We never stopped courting," she said without hesitation. A hush fell over the crowd, who heard it as profound wisdom and not the party-antic quip they were expecting.

The obvious secret for any partnership is to never take the relationship for granted. In a marriage, that might mean remembering red-letter days, bringing home flowers with a milestone in mind, paying a flattering compliment, or performing a ritual that is painted in the color adoration. The point is that noticeable passion attracts. Your passion can serve as a magnetic force to invite your customer's imagination out and onto the focus of your union.

Passion is the intersection where the best in a provider meets the best in a customer. A deliberate and cherished gift, it does more than yield loyalty on both sides; it harvests deep respect, admiration, and true devotion. Alliances with passion unleash innovation. "Passion," wrote world renowned cellist Yo-Yo Ma, "is one great force that unleashes creativity because if you are passionate about something, then you're more willing to take risks." "Courting" implies a "never take it for granted" energy that electrifies newness and supports a decorum of adoration. It affirms the connection and invigorates its inventiveness.

Most relationships with customers do not end with a storm of sound and fury. Most do not end in a fit of dissonance or from caustic conflict. Most "vanilla" to death. It is death by indifference, monotony, and negligence. Passion is the engine of enthusiasm that is never switched off. "Innovation equals change, and working through change requires massive investment of energy," wrote Doug Hall, founder of Eureka! Ranch. "The only way you can sustain the energy required to commercialize a meaningfully unique idea is if you really love it."

Passion in a co-creation partnership has three parts (figure 8). First is zeal. Zeal is not an extravert word; however, it is an expression associated with a charisma that influences. It is defined as "the fervor or tireless devotion to a person or cause and a determination in its furtherance." It is a fire-starting device that lights up ideation and kindles break-throughs. The second part of passion is "circus"—the setting for fueling innovation with your customer. The final part in Secret 5 focuses on honor as a gerund, not a noun. Honoring is bringing a sense of nobility to the celebration of innovation—its performers, its performance, and its process.

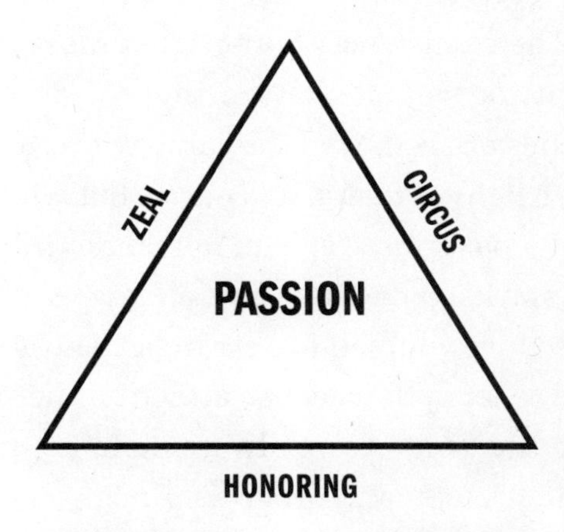

FIGURE 8. The components of passion

"Passion" was a reason given for the Inn at Sea Island (Georgia) being ranked the number 1 hotel in the United States in *U.S. News & World Report* in 2016, after winning the same ranking in 2014. "It is an unmistakable infectious energy," said Sea Island Company president Scott Steilen. "For our associates, it means confidently and competently shifting the disposition of each of our guests to one of pure delight." And the Inn at Sea Island type of passion is the antidote to spirit leeches.

One of the hazards of fishing swampy rivers is the risk of getting a leech. Unlike with many parasites, you cannot feel a leech attaching to your arm or leg. A ritual among river anglers is to always check for the bloodsuckers after emerging from the water. And the typical way to remove the slimy hitchhiker is with a lighted match or lighter.

Leeches suck the blood from their target; spirit leeches suck the energy and passion from theirs. Some spirit leeches are dark, removing optimism, hope, and confidence. Mention an opportunity and they can tell you why it's a mistake. Suggest a new approach to resolving a problem and they will tell you all the reasons it won't work. Some play the blame game or bring out the excuse use. Some are almost invisible, specializing in putting wet blankets on joy.

Spirit leeches are removed the same way real leeches are—with fire. Not a lighted match, of course, but with the warmth and energy of a passionate spirit. You do not inherit, acquire, or borrow a spirit of passion. You choose it much like you choose to introduce yourself to a stranger. Those who opt to be upbeat refuse to let spirit leeches attach to them. They know that breaking the "way we've always done it" norm can lead to enrichment, growth, and progress. And even introverts can muster up enough obvious passion to produce a customer grin!

Partnerships with power-full passion are personifications of honor. Symbolically, they bow or curtsy to each other. They are quick to affirm, equally quick to defend to an outsider. They bring a gifting mentality, always giving more than they expect to get. And they celebrate the raw side of innovation—the wild, audacious, partially baked, not-ready-for-prime-time creations.

When I facilitated an innovative-service creation session with a group of hospital leaders (who each had brought a key customer), the end-of-the-day comment most commonly heard was, "I have never felt more complete and more affirmed." It reminded me of the closing scene from the hit movie *Jerry Maguire*. Co-creation partnerships at their best are affirmations like that one: "You complete me."[1]

CHAPTER 13

Pass-I-On to Your Partnership

The spark of passion ignites the fuel for innovation.

—CRAIG GROESCHEL

You can tell you are about to meet zeal personified when a colleague's face lights up as he announces, "Let me get David for you." The coworker's animated look lodges your eager anticipation somewhere between "you are in for a treat" and "you ain't gonna believe this!"

Then, it happens. You come face to face with a person who has fallen hopelessly in love with his role!

My business partner and I were staying at a Marriott near Chicago, had finished a late afternoon hotel meeting with one client, and were en route to a nearby restaurant to meet another client for dinner. The restaurant was beyond walking distance but an insultingly short haul for a taxi or Uber driver. But the hotel van was available, and bell stand attendant David was to be our driver.

Now imagine this. You can "feel" David emotionally long before he shakes your hand. His enthusiasm is so apparent that his style and spirit meet you before he does. The first thing you notice is David's glowing Steinway smile—like he just unexpectedly encountered two long-lost boyhood friends. The second thing you notice is his gait—it's one of a man extremely eager to connect and raring to serve. Finally, you witness how his gusto infects every single soul within earshot with a robust case of the grins.

"Is it true I get the grand pleasure of being the chauffeur for you gentlemen tonight?" he asks incredulously, as if he were still pinching himself after winning a big prize! We felt like members of an exclusive club as we boarded his chariot of joy.

Our hotel meeting had gone quicker than we anticipated. Rather than abandoning our half-finished drinks, we elected to take them with us, especially since David was to be our designated driver.

"You gentlemen don't spill your grape juice," David teased as he made a sharp corner just shy of the restaurant. It was obvious he was crystal clear on the contents of our adult beverage cups and was having a blast accommodating our slight departure from customary van rules.

Depositing us at the restaurant, he gave us each a two-handed shake and his business card. "Would you gentlemen please call me when you finish dinner? I can be here in five minutes! And if you want to bring back a few buddies for a nightcap, we would love to take care of them as well." We literally wanted to rush through dinner just to get a return visit from the joyful spirit that accompanied David!

Let Your Zeal Invite Your Customer's Imagination

Inside your customer's imagination lie cool ideas, novel perspectives, and unique approaches. As provider, you are joining a person already committed to solving a problem, meeting a need, or achieving an aspiration. They invited you to their party. Your role is to convince their imagination you are just as enthused about achieving a result as they are. Your infectious attitude and contagious fervor will invite their imagination to join you. Passion is really three words: "pass-I-on"—passing on to your customer the wide open, high octane, genuine side of who you are. In the process, you are requesting their passion to connect.

> There is an energy field between people. When we reach out in passion, it is met with an answering passion and changes the relationship forever.
>
> —ROLLO MAY, *Love and Will*

So, what does zeal look like up close and personal? It can look like David. People with obvious zeal have countenances brighter than normal, their customer courtship is more confident than usual, and their connection is more captivating than typical. They parade zeal without "charging admission." When a politician shows you fervor, you put your hand on your wallet. When actors display enthusiasm, you get your money's worth. But the charm of a provider with zeal is just there for you to enjoy . . . no strings attached.

Providers with zeal seem liberated from the ties that bind most of us. They are not easily derailed or bothered by people who have turned bitter or cynical by their experiences on the planet. Their freedom is not an expression of rebellion or revolt. They show their joyful spirit because that is who they are, not because they have anything to prove or pitch.

What is it about this special breed of providers that turns them into Pied Pipers of sorts, making customers want to fall in line behind them in hopes that some of the joyful spirit might rub off? David provides us with a ready-made specimen to dissect, explore, and understand. David was having fun with us, not *for* us or *on behalf of* us. He was not a performer in pursuit of applause or a server eager to win a gratuity. He was just enjoying his role for the pure, simple pleasure it brought to both the served and the server. David obviously enjoyed the effect he was having. Yet it was clear he likely would have had a great time just "playing by himself." Watching David in action, you get the distinct impression that his mother forgot to tell him to be quiet.

This unbridled style has a magnetic power on customers. It draws out their higher self. Being in the presence of David-like providers makes customers feel good about themselves. It's difficult to misbehave or stay cranky in the company of a provider with zeal. Few among us want to drag storm clouds into the perpetually sunny skies of such life-forms.

Take Care of Eccentrics and Mad Scientists

The label "mad scientist" is a catchall phrase for the gifted, unconventional wild ducks that occasionally enter organizations. Remember how the son of Herb Peterson (Mr. Egg McMuffin) described his dad? "When my dad was let loose in a kitchen, he was half creative genius and half mad scientist." For most organizations, they bring mixed blessings. All mad scientists have common noble traits—they are brilliant, visionary, perfectionists, and passionately driven. They are also very challenging to work with, mercurial, extremely bull-headed, egotistical, irreverent, and once in a while, borderline crazy. Mad scientists ignore tidy rules of corporate civility in pursuit of their bold visions. They poke around in areas outside their sandbox and beyond their pay grades. They try most leaders' patience and can embarrass their team members who are seeking to make a good impression.

Every progressive organization needs a few mad scientists. They can make us better and more vigorous. Sure, they are complex, challenging, and downright difficult. But they can springboard an organization to greatness. Of course, they can make us wring our hands and shake our head. They can also ensure our advancement and competitiveness. Remember, how you treat these eccentrics can telegraph to the rest of the organization how much you really value the untraditional thinking needed for innovation. And sometimes these mad scientists happen to be your customer. The punch line is acceptance. Read the "remember" part again.

Co-creation partnerships are characterized by complete acceptance. Being effective at demonstrating complete acceptance fosters a spirit of inquiry on a level emotional playing field—a relationship with unrestricted access and involvement. And the byproduct of complete acceptance is the gift of courage—a crucial component for discovery, understanding, and true learning. Become famous for being a guardian of acceptance. Think of the role like protecting a super bright, talented kid brother from insults just because he sometimes acts silly.

I was working with a financial services company seeking to create a new service for their high net worth clients. I suggested they bring in a few of these clients and work with them to ensure it served the company's revenue goals while meeting a true customer aspiration. Many of these attendees were well-known, prominent leaders. It had the feel of a board meeting. I insisted they select one client famous for his eccentric behavior and style. When he arrived, he was coolly welcomed and the company leaders noticeably barely tolerated his unconventional manner.

About an hour into the two-hour meeting, I asked Mr. Eccentric to change seats with me at the head of the table and I moved to the side. I then asked him, "What have we missed in this discussion, George? What do you see that we may have overlooked?" It was like a reincarnation of Albert Einstein took over. His clear, clever wisdom came pouring out, much to the chagrin and incredulity of the financial services company leaders. With his astute intervention, not only did the group together craft a new solution in a matter of minutes, but the company leaders were asking George to join them for their next innovation session. Don't judge a person by his or her weirdness; there may be a genius inside.

Innocence Bests Intelligence in the Innovation Arena

This book started by stating that your customer's imagination is attracted out or is invited out. And we tip the scale by deliberately letting the majority of our five secrets be steered by who we are, not by what we do. When the secrets Curiosity, Trust, and Passion were unpacked, the concepts of authenticity, genuineness, and openness—the features we associate with innocence—were all in the spotlight. Here is a powerful example.

When John Longstreet (remember him as Mr. Harvey Hotel?) was the mayor of Plano, Texas, he and his city council had been wrestling with an issue for several meetings. Neither the council nor the staff could come up with a solution agreeable to the majority of the council members, so they tabled the issue. Not long after that, Mayor John spoke with the third graders at Razor Elementary School, something he periodically did throughout the school district. His subject was how city government was structured, how it worked, and how the citizens fit in as customers. After his presentation the teacher told John she wanted the students to take on a realistic case study having to do with the city. He told her he had just the issue, but requested that they share their outcome with him. And he gave the class the issue that the council had been unable to resolve. A few weeks later, he took the students' work with him to the city council. I will let John pick up the story from here.

"I told the council that I had a potential solution to the issue we had been wrestling with weeks before. After I reviewed the proposal with the council, they voted unanimously to adopt. I then informed them that the third graders of Razor Elementary had solved a problem that the Plano City Council had been unable to. A key lesson learned from this was to always look for imaginative answers in unusual places. The second lesson was, when you innocently have no biased or preconceived notions you can get better solutions."

Pass-I-On to Your Partnership: The Partnering Crib Notes

Somber, formal, staid business does not necessitate attitudes and actions that reflect the same characteristics. Your imagination is not jam-packed with numbers, graphs, charts, and formulas; it is laced with colorful pictures and not-of-this-world ideas. Your being in the middle of your imagination turned on is not like a boardroom; it's like a candy shop. Bring that same inside world to the outside. Think of it like childbirth. Some people choose to have a midwife in their home for baby delivery because it brings an infant into the world without bright operating-room lights and people in stark white uniforms with forceps and rubber gloves. Whether that is the path you would choose for childbirth is not the point; it is the logic behind that choice that points to fruitful imagination in the making. Birthing ideas needs your energy, an exciting context of joy, and a spirit of encouraging acceptance.

Passionate connections provoke passionate responses. And it is magical! Philosopher Goethe called it "boldness" and said, "Whatever you can do, or dream you can, begin in boldness. Boldness has genius, power, and magic in it. Until one is committed, there is hesitancy, the chance to draw back, always ineffectiveness. The moment one definitely commits oneself, then Providence moves, too. All sorts of things occur to help one that would never otherwise have occurred."

Your passion is waiting for your courage to catch up.

—ISABELLE LAFLÈCHE

CHAPTER 14

Bring In the Cirque de l'Imagination

Innovation comes when the wrong things are used in the wrong way at the wrong time but by the right people.

—NIELS BOHR, NOBEL PRIZE–WINNING PHYSICIST

Disney theme parks leave me happy and joyful; Cirque du Soleil performances leave me stunned and in complete awe. Disney is an enchanting experience; Cirque du Soleil is like-nothing-else amazing. Disney is warmly clever; Cirque is ingenuity on steroids.

Cirque du Soleil performances make you want to eat the icing and skip the cake. Every one of their twenty-plus different performances in almost three hundred cities, from *The Beatles LOVE* in Las Vegas to *Varekai* in Vienna, is laced with color, acrobatics, dance, and over-the-top music. It is a sensory menagerie. There is little predictable about any performance. Instead, you get head-turning surprise every few minutes. Consider the next encounter you have with your customer aimed at tapping imagination for an innovative solution. What if you approached it as a performance, not as a meeting? What if it were a circus of imagination?

Imagination is accessed in two ways—it is invited and it is attracted. Invited is like a printed request to attend a party;

attracted is more like the bakery that pumps the aroma of cookies in the oven into the street nearby. Much of this book has focused on inviting your customer to unleash their imagination through crafting a relationship of respect, trust, and acceptance. The "Cirque de l'Imagination" is designed to attract imagination from wherever it can be found. And it is the *Animal House* of innovation.

There are many features that make a circus a fitting analogy. From the moment the circus ringmaster says, "Ladies and gentlemen, children of all ages . . . ," you know you are in a welcoming, classless environment. From the tease of the ticket taker to the simplicity of the sawdust floor, it is a scene of pure joy. When animals from faraway places parade before your eyes, you experience the world of imagination in a backdrop of magic. When trapeze aerialists put your heart in your throat, the otherworldness of their bravery leaves you inspired. And we often leave with a souvenir to remind us of our astonishing experience.

Bring On the Cotton Candy

Cotton candy is a metaphor for unique food for imagination. Cotton candy is simply a spun-sugar confection—liquified sugar, sometimes with food coloring added, is spun through tiny holes. In Australia it is called "fairy floss." Its magic is in its simplicity since it contains few ingredients and is served on a simple paper cone. Here are a few simple cotton candy-like techniques to add to the circus of the imagination.

RANDOMIZE STIMULATION

An ideation meeting with the leadership of a company that owned several hundred malls took an unexpected turn.

The meeting was with a group of tenants to brainstorm ways to create a new mall experience that would drive traffic into the stores. Ideas spun out of control when the marketing director had their cafeteria deliver a live crab to the meeting room. Throwing it in the middle of the table, he asked, "What does this crab say about our customer experience and how we need to respond?" (See the sidebar at the end of this chapter.)

ELEVATE INNOCENCE

A West Coast bank was working with a group of customers on a Saturday to reinvent their branches to become more like a fun watering hole for customers. The leader of the meeting arranged with an elementary school to bring a group of first and second graders to the meeting to help with their discussion. Each child was paired with a customer to start the ideation that then expanded to the total group. Years later, employees still talk about that experience.

START AT THE END

Remember the Aesop's fable where the crow wanted to drink from the water jug but the water was too low to reach? The crow brought the water up to him by dropping rocks in the jug until the water level was high enough to drink. Reversing the starting point can provide a fresh perspective that can lead to a novel solution.

GET USED TO ABSURDITY

A consultant was working with a manufacturing company that had a challenge with turnover and absenteeism among employees who performed mind-numbing, repetitive work not yet robotized. The consultant suggested first brainstorming famous historical characters and then selecting one through whose eyes to consider the turnover challenge. When Jack the Ripper was the chosen character, someone immediately suggested Jack would cut off the legs of the factory workers so they could not leave. The absurd idea led to the decision to recruit more employees with physical challenges since their turnover records were much better than employees without physical challenges.

Send In the Clowns

"I remember in the circus learning that the clown was the prince, the high prince," wrote Roberto Benigni. "I always thought that the high prince was the lion or the magician, but the clown is the most important." The sentiment works for innovation. When children have a backyard birthday party, they don't invite aerialists or acrobats, they include a clown. It is a catalyst for innocent ideation and unfiltered joy. The concept can include creating what entrepreneur and master disruptor Miki Agrawal calls "containers of playfulness." These are deliberate steps to ramp up liberty of viewpoints and welcoming mats for wackiness.

Clowns are the ambassadors of silly. They make us think anything is possible and everything is okay. For the circus, they are sent in after a dramatic trapeze act or a daring knife-throwing act to signal to the audience that the circus is fundamentally about ingenious fun. Clowns are used in rodeos to distract the bull so the bull rider can escape after being thrown. They signal to the audience, "Hey, this might seem serious and scary but it is all about entertaining fun!"

It starts with taking a feature from table 1 and brainstorming ways it might directly apply to the customer's issue or challenge.[1]

1. Healthier	13. Quieter	25. Divided into parts
2. Instructional	14. Greener	26. Done alone
3. Faster	15. Smaller	27. Completely tailored
4. Slower	16. Bolder	28. Done in reverse
5. Smarter	17. Entertaining	29. Done remotely
6. Safer	18. Mysterious	30. Done while you wait
7. Romantic	19. Elegant	31. Done with a guide
8. Funnier	20. More invisible	32. More patriotic
9. Five star	21. More magical	33. More feminine/ masculine
10. More responsive	22. More efficient	34. More neighborly
11. More inclusive	23. More cultured	35. Done completely alone
12. A new application	24. Eliminated	

TABLE 1. What if it were . . .

McDonald's made their quick-service restaurant *smaller*, which enabled it to fit in airports and shopping centers. Arm & Hammer found a *new application* of their baking soda product and came out with a toothpaste. Home Depot made their customers *smarter* by adding do-it-yourself workshops. Quick-service restaurants have made service *faster* through apps that let customers place orders *remotely*. Hotels have enabled guest check-in to be *done completely alone* by providing phone apps for remote check-in and keyless room entry with the smartphone.

Add a Wild Sideshow

Traveling carnivals were not complete without sideshows. When I was a kid, we called them freak shows because of their propensity to include very odd people and animals. There were fire eaters, sword swallowers, and daredevil shows featuring motorcycles and sky-high dives into tiny pools. They were a unique, creative opportunity to witness the wild side. Every Cirque du Soleil show has some component that borders on the weird, even grotesque. Innovation needs that same type of freedom to explore rarely visited corners of our imaginations. Table 2 is a more advanced version of the previous exercise from my book *Take Their Breath Away.*[2] It involves choosing a character from the list and applying it to the customer's challenge.

A large law firm asked me to help them think out of the box about ways their client experience could be more positively memorable. They decided to use their lobby and reception area as their initial target of focus. And they elected to involve their clients in idea generation. They chose ten items from table 2 and put each on a separate index card that read, "We want to make your reception area a better experience and we need your ideas. Using the phrase on the card, write on the back one idea we should consider." Each client was given one card as they arrived for an appointment. The result? A "bird's eye view" (number 35) became a bird cage with love birds in the lobby, a "type of food" (number 25) became a giant gumball machine with a bowl of shiny pennies beside it, a "part of a circus" (number 38) became a popcorn machine in the waiting area, and a "piece of furniture" (number 20) became a cowhide-covered armchair that quickly turned into a topic of conversation.

ARTS	LIFESTYLE	ODD VIEWS	FAMOUS PEOPLE
1. Character in a movie	13. Other political party	26. You're the product	39. Military hero
2. Cartoon character	14. Occupation	27. You're the process	40. Comedian
3. Song title	15. Kitchen appliance	28. Kid's perspective	41. Politician
4. Subject of a painting	16. Room in the house	29. The other gender	42. Movie star
5. Colored differently	17. Vacation site	30. Customer's view	43. Inventor
6. Prop in a play	18. Make/type of car	31. Competitor's CEO	44. Villain
7. Musical instrument	19. Family oddity	32. Worst nightmare	45. Prize winner
8. Name of a band	20. Piece of furniture	33. Dream come true	46. Your biggest hero
9. Type of dance	21. Mode of transportation	34. Wild inventor	47. News reporter
10. Well-known story	22. Computer program	35. Bird's eye view	48. Favorite author
11. Book title	23. Gossip column	36. It's alive!	49. Famous artist
12. Joke/cliché/ad	24. Recreation or sport	37. Guinness candidate	50. Superhero
	25. Type of food	38. Part of a circus	51. Favorite athlete

TABLE 2. And what if it were . . .

Join the Circus and Run Away with Ideas

The Big Apple Circus in Lincoln Center in New York City is a place of nostalgia overload. It is a rendition of the old-fashioned

Ringling Bros. and Barnum & Bailey type of circus that used to come through small towns by rail. The highlight of the circus was the performers who rode on the backs of fancy horses and invited small kids from the audience to help with their act. While there were obvious safety precautions at play, it was clear from the faces of the children they were "in the circus," not "at the circus." The packed audience were attracted, as they were vicariously in the middle of the ring with the children.

Comedian Johnny Carson was fond of saying, "Never follow an act with animals or children." It speaks to the charm and creativity of little kids. The director of the local ASPCA humane society also taught a Sunday school class for elementary-aged students. She asked for their help on Sunday in identifying creative ways to encourage families to adopt a dog. One student suggested that if a family adopted a dog plus donated to the humane society, they would get a free dog house. The director went to the local hardware store, and they agreed to build free dog houses of all sizes as a community service project.

But the next week the student (a.k.a. customer), after hearing about her teacher's arrangement with the hardware store, had another suggestion. Get the store to offer to put the new dog's name on the front of the dog house (or let a kid spray-paint it on with stencils). It proved to be a way for the hardware store to get customers into their store, so they placed all their dog supplies right beside the paint station at the back of the store for impulse buys. The humane society found homes for dogs, the customer got a free personalized dog house, and the store got more traffic—a win, win, win. How can you involve children with your customer ideation opportunity?

Bring In the Cirque de l'Imagination: The Partnering Crib Notes

The process of innovation is to get the noisy, logical left brain to hush up so the shy and quiet, creative right side can be heard. There are techniques like deferring judgment and freewheeling, and there are tricks like teasing the right brain out with a toy, child, or story. Forcing the brain to look at a feature (larger, smaller, etc.) helps focus the right brain to unleash ideas. Changing the venue can help us see challenges with a new perspective. Remember, the left brain will get a turn at judging the pragmatism and practicality of an idea. But if it speaks first, you will never get the gifts of the imagination on the right.

The greatest circus professional in history was P. T. Barnum. He said, "Clowns are the pegs on which the circus is hung." His quote was intended to anchor the circus to the innocence of a child, the same venue where innovation lives. Cirque de l'Imagination admits only children or people willing to play like children. Ticket, please!

Damn everything but the circus! Damn everything that is grim, dull, motionless, unrisking, inward turning, damn everything that won't get into the circle, that won't enjoy. That won't throw its heart into the tension, surprise, fear and delight of the circus, the round world, the full existence.

—E. E. CUMMINGS

FEATURES OF A CRAB AND THEIR IMPLICATIONS

- Rejuvenates a lost claw. We must develop backup service lines in case our primary line falters.
- Can see 360 degrees. We must improve our market intelligence.
- Can move slowly. We cannot afford this. We must downsize so we can react more quickly to the market.
- Has distinct features. We need to develop a distinctive package that differentiates our service more clearly.
- Is a scavenger. We need to allocate resources to see what other uses and markets we can find for our services.

CHAPTER 15

Nobilize Honoring

No amount of ability is of the slightest avail without honor.
—ANDREW CARNEGIE

Two things I remember about my very first suit. It was a powder blue suit—perfect for Easter Sunday church dress-up. And the whole experience was a "big boy" event. I was seven years old. Joseph N. Neel's menswear in Macon, Georgia, was a two-hour drive from my rural hometown, and we visited only every August to buy school clothes. But this purchase required a special spring journey.

The "big boy" event started with the salesperson pulling up a chair in front of me at my eye level. He shook my hand and introduced himself by his first name, not "Mr." Without a single glance at my dad, he asked me about my favorite color. And my second favorite color. He asked me about my hobbies and wanted to know my best friend's name. We were pals in a matter of minutes. I walked out of the store very tall with a suit in my favorite color, a white dress shirt, a pair of shoes, and a tie in my second favorite color. Did I mention that I was seven?

Cherish Innovation through Honoring

Co-creation partnerships live and work in the playpen of ideas. Their "what ifs" can provoke wild and wacky silliness. The "partially baked" dimensions of input in this kitchen of kooky can leave its chef vulnerable to criticism or, at a minimum, skepticism. Its welcoming walls should be a host to the thin-skinned as well as the "tough guys." It should be an arena where the referee comes in late. It means a setting that evidences respect. And honoring is an action verb in the realm of respect.

Customers adore service connections with respect. Respectful service—experiences filled with admiration—starts and ends with a devotion to customers. It is affirmation laced with authenticity and awe. It is like a random act of kindness, only respectful service is not random; it is perpetual. When the R&D group at pioneering company Medtronic is stumped on a medical device innovation, they invite in patients who have had success with previous Medtronic products to talk about their experiences. Medtronic leaders claim the mutual-admiration meeting has contributed to many breakthroughs. It emanates from the company's mission: "We collaborate with others to take on healthcare's greatest challenges." They live it in the lab, not just in the marketplace.

Victoria's Secret Catalog (VSC) was a fun client of mine a number of years ago. Under the brilliant leadership of then CEO Cindy Fields, the company's revenue grew from $50 million to $800 million. It was also a time the company elevated its emphasis on the customers' experiences with their call center, not just the merchandise customers purchased.

One component of their "voice of the customer" initiative was to hold focus-group sessions with a group of customers who were chosen because they had recently bought and/or returned VSC merchandise. The first focus group was attended by all the senior leadership, including Cindy. At the end of the session, customers were given a gift, and while they got a tour of the facility in Columbus, Ohio, the executives who watched the focus group worked on ways to translate insights gained into actions or, in some cases, a wakeup call to get more intelligence. It was the kick-off of an initiative that enfolded customers into the internal operations of the company.

The highlight of the first focus-group session was inviting the customers at the end of their tour to have lunch in the employee cafeteria. Prior to their arrival, the word was quickly passed that a group of customers was coming to the cafeteria. As the customers entered the large cafeteria, the entire room erupted in a lengthy standing ovation. It was powerful, and it was affirming! In the words of one employee in the room, "This makes my challenging work worth it." And in the words of one of the customers in the room, "I have never felt more respected in my whole life. I don't want this relationship to ever be over."

What was special about this working celebration? It was egalitarian. The CEO was at the same level as the customers and her employees. In fact, instead of having me lead the session, she asked me to teach the director of creative (the woman in charge of their famous catalog) to lead the focus-group meeting so everyone could learn how to replicate this experience. Customers were not treated as visitors but as an integral part of VSC's regular business operation, their feedback valued and their ideas cherished. And they created a way for their contribution to be honored in a profound and awe-inspiring manner.

Think of a respectful approach as "grandmother-style service." Grandmothers spoil you just because they get a kick out of it—remembering your favorite everything, always giving you a little bit extra, and cheering you up when others chastise. Grandmothers believe you are still terrific even after your parents grounded you. Delivering respect is the service equivalent of being your customers' grandmas.

Make Honoring Nonjudgmental

For several years, I served on the faculty of Marriott's Executive Education Program—a weeklong residential learning experience for high-potential general and regional managers held quarterly at the Wye River Conference Center on the eastern shore of Maryland. It was a historical setting for learning about partnership since it was the site where President Bill Clinton facilitated a peace agreement between Israel's Benjamin Netanyahu and the PLO's Yasser Arafat.

Marriott had just acquired hotel properties from Whitbread Hotels, a UK hospitality company. The cultural personalities of Whitbread and Marriott could not have been more different. That reality surfaced loudly during an animated discussion in the morning class. The Whitbread GM aimed a sarcastic, biting tease point blank at a Marriott GM. The entire class went silent for an uncomfortably long time. You could see the Whitbread GM was confused at the reaction to his comment, one wholly appropriate in the more acerbic British culture in which he lived and worked.

At the first break, three Marriott GMs pulled the Whitbread GM aside. I could hear bits and pieces of their assertive conversation. Bottom line, the message was clear—we do not speak to one another in a way that is judgmental or sarcastic. The Marriott culture is laced with allegiance to kindness, supportiveness, and authenticity. They take seriously Edwards Deming's profound wisdom to drive fear out of the workplace.

Partnerships in the era of innovation and settings of imagination treat fear as a significant detriment to ingenuity. Fear shackles risk-taking; judgment bridles experimentation. Never forget you are dealing with your customer's imagination—a part of their anatomy that has likely been bullied by its fraternal twin on the other side of the brain. You need to be its champion and advocate. More importantly, you need to serve as its friendly shepherd, clearing the way for safe transport to your customer's challenges and aspirations in search of resolution, solution, and creation.

Co-creation partnerships are free-idea zones because they are neighborhoods of acceptance and goodness.

Make Honoring Egalitarian

My wife and I were having lunch with friends at one of the three restaurants at the renowned Culinary Institute of America (CIA) in Hyde Park, New York. The CIA is the training ground for the world's most celebrated chefs. One of our party of four ordered lamb chops. The waitress (who was graduating the next day to become the sous chef at the Four Seasons Hotel in Philadelphia) advised her, "The chef recommends this entree be prepared medium rare. But do you have a different opinion?"

I was deeply struck by the comment's elevation of the customer to equal footing with a chef who was, in fact, a professor of chefs. It was mixed with sincere respect. It was a moment we all talked about throughout the meal. And it caused me to realize the delicious spirituality of partnerships and their power to invite commitment, compassion, and boldness. Partnerships at their best are not about contracts, control, and compromises; they are about respectful connections that enliven, ennoble, and enchant. They are never static or set; rather, they are always evergreen and growing.

"Egalitarian" is a fifty-nine-cent word that means placing a priority on equality. It is the foundation of our "all are created equal" democracy. It is the guiding principle of commerce at its finest—equal value fairly exchanged. And it is the foundation of a partnership and all relationships that last.

Co-creation partnerships are egalitarian and are also populated by people with a bias for mutual advocacy. A prepared-frozen meal company, having recently been acquired by a large multinational corporation, needed to prove to their new owners they could become cutting edge. As they assessed opportunities for efficiency improvements, they discovered a major concern—their packaging line was a single line requiring twenty employees to pack boxes. With high labor costs and high turnover, the VP of engineering needed a partner with deep expertise in packaging to collaboratively design an automated process. They selected Westrock.

The partnership started with a clear focus, the right players, a budget, and a detailed, aligned work plan and agreements. The multi-week process involved senior leaders, engineers, designers, technical specialists, and machinists from both companies. Spirits were high as all were passionately involved in cracking the code to solve this unique challenge. When the new packing lines and box design were rolled out, high fives abounded as they celebrated the deep, trusting relationship they had forged. They had become extensions of each other's teams and began planning more projects together.

Co-creation partnerships are laser focused on "keeping the junk out of the juice," as a senior leader at Ultimate Software once told me. Partnerships with juice are those with vitality and forward zeal to accomplish a mission or goal. Partnerships with honor nurture the partnership's longevity with the meticulousness of a bonsai caretaker. And they celebrate its soul through faithful attention and everyday goodness.

Sursy Your Partner

I just found this new word. And it has nothing to do with square dancing! "Sursy"! Now, before you go look it up, let me give you a small clue. It is the physical version of a random act of kindness. It can turn even the dourest countenance into a jovial wide-angle beam.

My wife and I rented a rustic cabin in Maggie Valley, North Carolina, while visiting a close friend in the hospital nearby. Arriving at streamside cabin number 3 at Twin Brook Resorts, we unpacked the car. When the ice chest got its turn, we encountered a sursy! Sitting in the refrigerator was a fresh sock-it-to-me cake with a cheery note on top. "We know you have been traveling and thought this would come in handy." It was signed by the owners—Lyndon and Greg. We were thrilled!

So, now you know. A sursy is an unexpected gift. It is tangible evidence of generosity unassociated with an event that usually warrants a gift—like a birthday or a gift-giving holiday. It is an old Southern word, but even some forever, dyed-in-the-wool Southerners have never heard of it. Regardless of the moniker, it should be an ever-present resident in the manner we partner with customers. The spontaneous component mimics that same element that makes innovation effective.

Giving a "sursy" is a lot like "dating" your customer. Remember what it was like to be new in a special love relationship. You were always looking for acts of magnanimity to remind the love of your life of his or her importance to you. You never took that person for granted. You celebrated small moments and you bestowed sursies upon this person—even without knowing that word. What if your customers received similar treatment? Start thinking about what sursy you might want to select for your customer! It will show you care; it will honor their contribution.

A sursy is a form of gratitude. When your passion invites your customer's imagination to come out to co-create, it is a two-way street. It is also your customer inviting you in. It is like a friend who says, "Next time, I'm buying." It is the epitome of co-laboring. That invitation to your customer's imagination neighborhood warrants an expression of gratitude. You don't have to bring wine, but it is important to say "thank you" in some form. "Gratitude is not only the greatest of virtues," wrote Cicero, "but the parent of all others."

Nobilize Honoring: The Partnering Crib Notes

Use "sir" and "ma'am" to people you do not normally address in that manner. Thank someone who never gets expressions of gratitude—the custodian in the bathroom, the cashier in the checkout line, the invisible and taken-for-granted maintenance people. Be a proactive guardian of your customers' dignity. Respectful service entails an extra helping of help, an enduring act of benevolence, and a sincere interest in making a difference in the welfare of those around you. Give for the sheer joy of giving. A thing is bigger for being shared. Be famous for your generosity; be even more renowned for your gratitude.

Honoring is the communication of respect. It comes in countless forms. We honor with ceremony, ritual, and eloquent elocution. Awards, plaques, and decorations publicize our expressions. But respect is about the manner in which a person is treated that telegraphs valuing and admiration. In the words of Eliza Doolittle in the hit musical *My Fair Lady*, "The difference between a lady and a flower girl is not how she behaves, but how she is treated."[1]

Nothing great in the world has ever been accomplished without passion.

—W. F. HEGEL

Continuing the Adventure

It's time to say goodbye, but I think goodbyes are sad and I'd much rather say hello. Hello to a new adventure.

—ERNIE HARWELL

My grandmother was a great wild-game cook. At her table during my childhood, my family enjoyed wild turkey, venison, wild boar, squirrel, and even an occasional opossum. One of my favorite dishes was her rabbit stew (hasenpfeffer). She used an antique recipe that had as its first instruction: "First, get a rabbit." The recipe for co-creating with customers begins the same way—first, get a customer.

Your adventure begins by communicating to your marketplace that you are a resource for experimentation and thus open to collective discovery. It signals you are willing to be courageous and adventurous instead of betting solely on the "tried and true" and "proven results." Ideas cannot be stockpiled nor creativity inventoried. It is a part of the "on faith" section of the balance sheet, right along with advertising, new ventures, and world-class customer service.

When customers acknowledge or imply their uncertainty about a clear path to their aspirations, it should also be a welcome sign of their search for a partner willing to work with them, not just on their behalf. Consider it an affirming gesture, and demonstrate your enthusiasm as well as your humility. An invitation to partner for innovation is not a sales pitch any more than you would sell a person on being your friend or spouse. Features and benefits might not have the same influence capability as curiosity, grounding, discovery, trust, passion, and a willingness to discover together.

Build the relationship before you start crafting ideas. Clarify the collective focus and agree on the guardrails before you begin whiteboarding a plan. This is not drive-by innovation; it must be unfolded thoughtfully. Rushing to the punchline not only risks leaving unused genius and ignored imagination in your path, it also hazards leaving your customer back there as well. The goal is not just a successful outcome; it is one that works for all. That requires the amalgamation of the needs and talents of all constituents involved and a clear cognizance of all people impacted. And when success is underway, don't forget to celebrate your collaboration and express your gratitude for all contributions.

Let's do one last review before we bid adieu. Why this book? Organizations need breakthrough products, services, and solutions to effectively compete. They need the customer's imagination to ensure the discovery of innovative and valued offerings. How? Accessing the customer's imagination requires a co-creation partnership that invites and attracts creative contributions. A co-creation partnership takes 1) curiosity that uncovers insight, 2) grounding that promotes clear focus, 3) discovery that fosters risk-taking and experimentation, 4) trust that safeguards partnership purity and wholeness, and 5) passion that inspires energized generosity. And the payoff? The journey leads to ingenious outcomes and a customer who emerges as an advocate.

Writing this book has been a great experience for me. In a profound and personal way, the process has helped me sort out what I believe about partnering and collaborative innovation. For much of my professional life, my vision of the innovation process was sort of the "Edison in a lab" image—a lone inventor toiling late into the night. Despite the appeal of synergism and the magnetism of "two heads together," that rugged individualism and solo pioneering spirit had a romantic appeal.

But a turning point came when my son came down the hospital hallway with tears rolling down his face and a glow on his countenance to announce, "We have a perfect baby girl, and her name is Kaylee Marie." My wife's middle name is Marie. It was a magical moment of announcing a creation that came from a partnership, the miracle of birth replicated by countless couples every day all over the world. Yet, despite its ordinariness from a world view, it was clearly a moment of exhilaration for him and the grandparents, family, and friends who witnessed his excited announcement.

"Imagination is more important than intelligence," said Albert Einstein, arguably the twentieth century's most intelligent person. "For knowledge is limited to all we now know and understand, while imagination embraces the entire world, and all there ever will be to know and understand." As customers, our imagination applied to a challenge is much the same. Intelligent service makes us feel secure, but applications that source our imagination make us swoon. Smart service builds our confidence; solutions with imagination make our heart skip a beat.

The by-product of a customer partnership focused on innovation is more than loyalty or advocacy. It is a deep, abiding bond that emerges from risking together, being authentic and vulnerable together, and solving or inventing together. It is a microcosm of interpersonal relationships at their finest, a model for the best of democracy in action. It starts with the courageous act to more passionately connect. And it starts with a single encounter—your next one.

Only connect.

—E. M. FORSTER, *Howards End*

A Partnership Checkup

Partnerships are different from teams. Teams generally have someone in the role of leader; partnerships generally do not. Partnerships are relationships in which using your "I'm the boss" position is either ineffective or inappropriate. In some ways, partnerships are "marriages of equals" with a common vision and mutual values, but with different talents and/or resources. The objective is to use the relationship to effectively harness those unique talents to achieve shared goals.

This Partnership Checkup tool can be copied and used without permission.

Step One: Reflection

Whoa . . . you may have already scanned the following ten items and thought about it for a nanosecond and felt ready to go on to part two. If you are reading this when you have limited time to reflect, please put it aside and come back to it when you can focus . . . that might more likely be early on a Sunday morning, not on Monday afternoon!

Think about the important relationship you are using this Partnership Checkup to examine. If he/she/they were answering the following ten questions for you, what might they say?

1. How often do you go beyond what your customers or colleagues expect in a relationship?

2. How often do you do extras for customers or colleagues just for the heck of it?

3. How often do you take a loss to help out a customer or colleague?

4. What is your emotional reaction to missing a promised deadline? To delivering lower quality than you promised?

5. How do you usually react to customers or colleagues whose attitude you consider selfish or greedy?

6. How important is bringing your very best to key relationships? What would your previous partners say about this?

7. If your son or daughter (assume you have one if you do not) picked a business day at random and could secretly watch you in all your business relationships, what would he or she learn about your partnering behavior and attitude?

8. What are the areas in previous partnerships where you had difficulty sharing control?

9. In what areas of a partnership do you find it most difficult to be completely candid?

10. When an important partnership gets contentious or laced with conflict, how would your partner describe your typical approach to resolving differences?

Step Two: Improving Your Partnership

Provide short answers to the following questions. Then meet with your partner(s) and compare answers as a trigger to an improvement discussion.

1. Ways I uniquely benefit my partner are . . .
2. The unique benefit I gain most from my partner is . . .
3. The primary value(s) critical to our effectiveness is (are) . . .
4. My partner would probably describe me as . . .
5. My gut tells me we'd work better if I would *stop* or *start* . . .
6. I believe I irritate my partner most when I . . .
7. The consequence of my being more candid/frank is . . .
8. What this partnership is teaching me is . . .
9. We generally have our biggest conflicts about . . .
10. An area we have not talked about that we should is . . .

The Amazing, Technicolor, Super Cool Lemonade Stand

A STUDY GUIDE

Let's start with a pretend scenario. You are an enterprising junior high school student with a desire to make your start in the world of commerce with an innovative lemonade stand. Your competitors make ordinary lemonade and sell it from a simple stand on a high-traffic corner. You are convinced that your customers—thirsty passersby—have bottled up inside them some super cool ideas for disrupting the way lemonade is conceived and delivered. You need your customers' help.

1. Why is it important to change the lemonade stand game today? What can you gain by co-creating a lemonade stand with your customers?

   Consider the rewards you can attain at the end of a profitable summer. Think about the impact on your customers if you decide to do a lemonade stand again next summer. Don't forget the lemonade stand is long overdue for disruption and you are the one who can do it.

2. What are the realities of nurturing a co-creation partnership to recreate the lemonade stand? What is the

SWOT analysis (strengths, weaknesses, opportunities, and threats) for a revolutionary lemonade stand?

Consider the importance of great lemonade in your customers' lives. Think about the need for a new delivery process in the hurry-up world in which your customers live. Don't forget you are examining every component of the lemonade stand experience, from product to marketing to delivery. For example, what would Uber, Disney, or Amazon do with this challenge?

3. Your first step is to engage your customers in a partnership relationship, not merely a drive-by transaction. What can you say or do to help your customers want to join you in the co-creation process long enough to capture their imagination, not just their top-of-mind suggestions?

   Consider labeling it in a unique way (the Lemonade Dream) or having a fun poster or flyer to accompany your pitch. What can you provide as an inexpensive giveaway to intrigue your customer? What if you gave your customer a lemon carved in a funny face to hold during conversation? Use a stopwatch for a five-minute max conversation.

4. Let's assume you have convinced an enthusiastic lemonade customer to give you ten focused minutes. Your first step is to use curiosity to build trust in order to create a safe haven for their insights and ideas. What are ways you would begin that process?

   Consider what authentic curiosity might look and sound like to your customer. Identify three questions you might ask that are crafted to be deeply thought provoking. Don't forget to watch how your customers react to what you say or do as added evidence for your understanding.

5. There are lemonade stands and then there is *your* lemonade stand. Your next goal is to both elevate and sharpen your and your customers' focus on a new meaning of "lemonade stand." Your goal is to put the conventional on mute and turn up the volume on a unique meaning of your goal. How will you get your customers to think differently about what a lemonade stand can be?

   Consider taking "lemonade stand" to the Miss America-pageant level of "solving world hunger." Think about applying new eyes to your focus (think in terms of different color, shape, role models, metaphors, senses, etc.). Don't forget that attracting ideas starts with making that pursuit fun, interesting, and enchanting.

6. Now, the hard work begins . . . the heavy-duty discovery part! This is where you want to encourage your customer to take a few risks. That means helping them take their idea-generator to mental places it has not been in, at least not in public.

   Consider this: if you had a friend who was shy or overly cautious, what steps would you take to help this friend demonstrate courage? Apply those steps to your customer. Think about how you will model authenticity. Don't forget boldness and risk-taking are easier when accompanied by others being bold. Show your courage.

7. Vulnerability can sometimes make us suddenly cautious, like we might have gone a bit too far. You have encouraged your customer to "remove her or his shield";

it is now important to provide reassurance that you can be trusted. What are three ways in any relationship you can demonstrate trustworthiness? How can you get your customer to conclude that being genuine in front of you was the right move?

Consider the power of promise-keeping. Think about reaffirming an agreement made at the beginning of your relationship. Don't forget that making mistakes shows you are human; acknowledging mistakes demonstrates you are a courageous and compassionate human.

8. Great co-creation partnerships are noble affirmations of the best of who we are and a gallant pursuit of what we can be. What are ways you can demonstrate to your customer your gratitude for contribution? How can you celebrate your alliance?

Consider requesting your customers' email addresses, and send them your top ten most unique lemonade recipes. Give them a yellow balloon. Start a LemonLaughs e-newsletter with funny lemonade jokes or quotes. "If life gives you lemons, ask for tequila and salt" or "Squeeze the day" (okay, I'll stop!).

How was the lemonade?

Notes and References

Sources and works cited are in order of their appearance in the text. Examples not referenced here are from my consulting practice or personal experience or borrowed and used with permission from coworkers, clients, and colleagues.

Beginning the Adventure

1 Peter F. Drucker, *The Practice of Management* (New York: Heinemann, 1954), 39.

Introduction: Welcome to Your Customer's Imagination

1 Smith, "The Checkered (in a Good Way) History of Vans Shoes," Smith Journal, June 29, 2017, smithjournal.com.

2 Alexis Fournier, "My Starbucks Idea: An Open Innovation Case Study," Braineet, March 20, 2019, Braineet.com.

3 Tom Peters, *Liberation Management: Necessary Disorganization for the Nanosecond Nineties* (New York: Knopf, 1992), 740.

4 Christine Crandell, "Customer Co-Creation Is the Secret Sauce to Success," *Forbes*, June 10, 2006, Forbes.com.

5 Chip R. Bell, *Customers as Partners: Building Relationships That Last* (San Francisco: Berrett-Koehler Publishers, 1994), 2.

SECRET 1: CURIOSITY

Chapter 1: Practice Eccentric Listening

1 Stephen Covey, *The 7 Habits of Highly Effective People* (New York: Simon & Schuster, 1989).

2 Chip R. Bell and Heather Shea, *Dance Lessons: Six Steps to Great Partnerships in Business and Life* (San Francisco: Berrett-Koehler Publishers, 1998), 116.

3 Dinah Eng, "How Maxine Clark Built Build-a-Bear," *Fortune*, March 19, 2012.

Chapter 2: Witness Your Customer through an Anthropologist's Lens

1 *Because of Winn-Dixie*, directed by Wayne Wang (Twentieth Century Fox, 2005), based on the book by Kate DiCamillo.

2 "Jimmy Carter: Presidential Medal of Freedom Announcement of Award to Margaret Mead," The American Presidency Project, January 19, 1979, accessed October 20, 2019, https://www.presidency.ucsb.edu/node/250392.

3 George Bradt, "How P&G Became 'Part of Walmart,'" Cornerstone International Group, August 9, 2018, https://www.cornerstone-group.com/2018/08/09/how-pg-became-part-of-walmart/.

4 Linda A. Hill, Greg Brandeau, Emily Truelove, and Kent Lineback, *Collective Genius, The Art and Practice of Leading Innovation* (Brighton, MA: Harvard Business Review Press, 2014), 75.

5 William C. Taylor, "Get Out of that Rut and Into the Shower," *New York Times*, August 13, 2006.

6 Mary Bellis, "The History of the Frisbee," ThoughtCo., January 15, 2019, https://www.thoughtco.com/history-of-the-frisbee-4072561.

Chapter 3: Make Customer Inquiry Unleashed and Unfiltered

1 *In Search of Excellence: The Movie*, distributed by Enterprise Media (Nathan/Tyler Productions, 1985), based on *In Search of Excellence* by Tom Peters and Robert Waterman (New York: Harper and Row, 1982).

2 John A. Byrne, "The Fast Company Interview: Jeff Immelt," *Fast Company*, July 1, 2005.

SECRET 2: GROUNDING

Chapter 4: Put Insight in Focus

1 John R. DiJulius, *The Relationship Economy: Building Stronger Customer Connections in the Digital Age* (Austin, TX: Greenleaf Book Group Press, 2019).

2 Edward de Bono, *Lateral Thinking: Creativity Step by Step* (New York: Harper Colophon, 2015), 107.

3 Dorothy Leonard, "The Limitations of Listening," sidebar in Anthony W. Ulwick, "Turn Customer Input into Innovation," *Harvard Business Review*, December 2002.

4 Theodore Levitt, *The Marketing Imagination* (New York: Free Press, 1986), 8.

5 Coleman Wood, "The Original Chicken Sandwich," The Chicken Wire, May 5, 2017, TheChickenWire.chick-fil-a.com.

6 Jacques Bughin, "Three Ways Companies Can Make Co-Creation Pay Off," McKinsey & Company, December 2014.

Chapter 5: Construct Value-Based Guardrails

1 "The Little Sandwich with a Huge Impact—The Egg McMuffin," McDonald's Newsroom, June 3, 2016, McDonalds.com.

2 Jeff Toister, *Getting Service Right: Overcoming the Hidden Obstacles to Outstanding Customer Service* (Toister Performance Solutions, 2019), servicerightbook.com.

Chapter 6: Be the Partnership Warranty

1 Michael Peterson, "Investigator: Failed Clamp Caused Circus Accident," CNN, May 7, 2014, CNN.com.

2 Shep Hyken, *The Convenience Revolution: How to Deliver a Customer Service Experience that Disrupts the Competition and Creates Fierce Loyalty* (Shippensburg, PA: Sound Wisdom, 2018).

SECRET 3: DISCOVERY

Chapter 7: Create an Incubation Alliance

1 Chip R. Bell and John R. Patterson, *Wired and Dangerous: How Your Customers Have Changed and What to Do about It* (San Francisco: Berrett-Koehler Publishers, 2011), 100.

2 Gordon MacKenzie, *Orbiting the Giant Hairball: A Corporate Fool's Guide to Surviving with Grace* (New York: Viking Press, 1998).

Chapter 8: Be All . . . There

1 Glenn Rifkin, "How Harley Davidson Revs Up Its Brand," *strategy+business*, October 1, 1997.

2 Peter Senge, *The Fifth Discipline: The Art and Practice of a Learning Organization* (New York: Doubleday/Currency, 1990).

3 Seth Godin, "How to Get Your Ideas to Spread," TED2003, February 2003.

4 Texas Bix Bender, *Don't Squat with Yer Spurs On!* (Layton, UT: Gibbs Smith, 2009), 74.

Chapter 9: Stretch Imagination Chi

1 Laura Geggel, "Why Do Cats Stretch So Much?" reporting on research of Andrew Cuff, Live Science, April 21, 2016.

2 Eric Stirgus, "Morehouse Professor Hailed for Babysitting Student's Child in Class," AJC, March 3, 2019, AJC.com.

3 Seth Godin, "Innovation Is Guts Plus Generosity," *Seth's Blog*, August 13, 2019.

4 Clayton M. Christensen, Karen Dillon, Taddy Hall, and David S. Duncan, *Competing Against Luck: The Story of Innovation and Customer Choice* (New York: HarperBusiness, 2016).

5 Edward de Bono, *Lateral Thinking: Creativity Step by Step* (New York: Harper Colophon, 2015).

SECRET 4: TRUST

1 Linda Tischler, "He Struck Gold on the Net (Really)," *Fast Company*, May, 31, 2002.

Chapter 10: Start Partnering with the Whole Truth

1 Carl Rogers, *A Way of Being* (Boston: Houghton-Mifflin, 1980).

2 Keith Hammond, "No Risk, No Reward," *Fast Company*, April 2000, 82–93.

Chapter 11: Set Innovation Working Agreements

1 Chip R. Bell and Marshall Goldsmith, *Managers as Mentors: Building Partnerships for Learning*, 3rd ed. (San Francisco: Berrett-Koehler Publishers, 2013), 137.

Chapter 12: Heed Caution Lights for Contracts

1 John J. Sherwood and John C. Glidewell, *Planned Renegotiation: A Norm-Setting OD Intervention*, paper no. 338 (Krannert Graduate School of Management, Institute for Research in the Behavioral, Economic, and Management Sciences, 1971).

2 Nancy Andreasen, *The Creative Brain: The Science of Genius* (New York: Dana Press, 2005).

SECRET 5: PASSION

1 *Jerry Maguire*, written and directed by Cameron Crowe (TriStar Pictures, 1996).

Chapter 14: Bring In the Cirque de l'Imagination

1 Chip R. Bell and John R. Patterson, *Customer Loyalty Guaranteed: How to Create, Lead, and Sustain Remarkable Customer Service* (New York: Adams Business, 2007), 8.

2 Chip R. Bell and John R. Patterson, *Take Their Breath Away: How Imaginative Service Creates Devoted Customers* (Hoboken, NJ: John Wiley & Sons, 2009), 50.

Chapter 15: Nobilize Honoring

1 George Bernard Shaw, *Pygmalion: A Play* (NY: Brentano, 1916), adapted as the Broadway play *My Fair Lady* in 1956 by Lerner and Loewe.

Thank You's

Book writing is an innovation partnership in its purest form. The final product reflects the benefits of the depths of interdependence. I am humbled by the creative and emotional support of those who have been involved with me in this co-creation adventure.

This book started with a rough, half-baked idea, evolved through many iterations, and benefitted from the wisdom of a world-class team. My friend Terry Kay, a renowned bestselling fiction author, told me that a book begins after the third draft. I can vouch for that truth. I am grateful for the patience and tenacity of my book writing team, who hung in there with me through version after version after version.

I first want to thank the many friends who provided me co-creation examples to consider for this book. Many are bestselling authors. Some include Shep Hyken, Joseph Michelli, Jeanne Bliss, Jay Baer, John DiJulius, Jeff Toister, Steve Curtin, John Longstreet, Dave Basarab, Tom Berger, Todd Gentry, Don Reggio, Tracey Artigue, Deana Larson, Ellison Thomas, Meghan Bell, Paul Cardis, and many others. I am also grateful to John Patterson, Lisa McLeod, Amanda Setili, Dave Basarab, Candace Sinclair, Ken Fracaro, and Kathy Scheiern for reading the draft and providing me with helpful feedback.

Berrett-Koehler Publishers is a co-creation partnership publisher. Unlike most publishers, where authors are viewed as suppliers, at Berrett-Koehler authors are intimately involved with every component of the bookmaking process. Transparency, candor, and shared control are key guardrails. There are many BK partners to thank. Of particular note are Valerie Caldwell, Edward Wade, Mike Crowley, Leslie Crandall, and Jeevan Sivasubramaniam. I would like to thank my world-class PR team at Weaving Influence, particularly Becky Robinson, Christy Kirk, Erica Hopper, Kelly Edmiston, and Rachel Royer. This is my fifth book launch with Weaving Influence. And I would like to thank my world-class copyeditor, Susan Berge, and book designer, Maureen Forys, both of Happenstance Type-O-Rama.

Three people deserve special recognition.

Leslie Stephen served as my vernacular engineer extraordinaire. She was there around the clock making wise suggestions, rearranging paragraphs, critiquing messaging, and ensuring the book reflected clarity instead of author mumblings, inventiveness instead of plain vanilla prose. She delivered raw candor without bruising my ego. She communicated authentic affirmation that made me want to write all night long. This is our ninth book together, a commentary on the triumph of our partnering.

Steve Piersanti served as my developmental editor. Steve reflects the epitome of the proper role of writing mentor—helping authors source and reveal the best of what their book is attempting to become and communicate. I think of Steve as a counsel to the muses who visited me in the middle of the night to bring amazing content; I was present to simply take dictation. This is my sixth book with Berrett-Koehler Publishers; Steve has coached me through several of them. Steve also founded the company in 1992.

Finally, the most important partner in my life, Nancy Marie Rainey Bell, gave me many precious gifts. Every writer births a book through the ancient process of sleepless nights and long stares at a blank computer screen interspersed with moments of insight and flow. She was there always as my cheerleader and confidante. She heard my doubts and shared my thrills. She listened to many "listen to this part" renditions and always made me feel as if I could teach Hemingway, Austen, and Rowling how to write. This soul-searching creation was made worthier through her inspiration.

To all my partners . . . thanks.

Index

About the Author

Chip's life as a writer began when Mrs. Ridley gave him an A+ on his eleventh-grade essay titled "The Sex Life of a Coat Hanger." He spent much of his youth in the woods of his family's farm in South Georgia masquerading as a little boy since he was a superhero in his imagination.

He charmed his graduate school professors into giving him good grades (Vanderbilt and George Washington University), thus preparing him for a career as a renowned keynote speaker. Global Gurus in 2020 ranked him for the sixth year in a row in the top three keynote speakers in the world on customer service. Chip's keynotes focus on innovative service, customers as partners, and mining your customer's imagination. His clients have included companies known for great customer service, including the Ritz-Carlton Hotels, USAA, Capital One, Southwest Airlines, Verizon, GE, Bayer, Cadillac, IBM, Marriott, and Harley-Davidson.

He spent about twenty years on a one-year tour in Vietnam as an infantry unit commander with the elite 82nd Airborne. He returned to the States with a chest full of medals for valor and enough really cool war stories to occupy a lifetime of dinner parties. Chip also served as a guerilla tactics instructor at the US Army Infantry School.

After eight years in the corporate world as the director of organization development and training for a large bank, Chip launched a consulting practice in 1980 focused on creating cultures that support long-term customer loyalty. Many of his award-winning, best-selling books center on innovative, value-unique customer experiences, including *Take Their Breath Away*, *Magnetic Service*, *The 9½ Principles of Innovative Service*, *Managing Knock Your Socks Off Service*, *Service Magic*, *Sprinkles*, and *Kaleidoscope*. He worked with legendary Academy Award–winning Warner Bros. cartoonist Chuck Jones to coauthor *Beep Beep! Competing in the Age of the Road Runner*. He also coauthored *Magnetic Service* with his son, Bilijack.

He still thinks he might be a superhero or at least a rock star since he once opened for the Backstreet Boys. Chip's favorite color is purple; his favorite food is Mexican; his favorite music is Italian opera and classic country. He has been married for over fifty years to Dr. Nancy Rainey Bell, an attorney and graduate school professor, and has a son, a daughter-in-law, and three gorgeous, really smart granddaughters.

Chip can be reached at www.chipbell.com.

Contact Chip about his keynotes, workshops, webinars, and award-winning training programs.

Also by Chip R. Bell

Wired and Dangerous

How Your Customers Have Changed and What to Do about It

By Chip R. Bell and John R. Patterson

In an era of economic stress, rapid change, and social networking, customers are distracted and harder to please than ever. In *Wired and Dangerous*, Bell and Patterson provide a tested formula for restoring balance to the customer relationship by establishing what they call "Service Calm." The three steps to Service Calm draw on sophisticated psychological principles and are profound in application: Deal with Self, Deal with Customer, and Deal with Context.

Print paperback, ISBN 978-1-60509-975-0
PDF ebook, ISBN 978-1-60509-976-7
ePub ebook, ISBN 978-1-60509-977-4
Digital audio, ISBN 978-1-60994-933-4

Managers as Mentors, Third Ed.

Building Partnerships for Learning

By Chip R. Bell and Marshall Goldsmith

Managers as Mentors is a rapid-fire read that guides leaders in helping associates grow in today's tumultuous organizations. The third edition places increased emphasis on the mentor acting as a learning catalyst with the protégé rather than simply handing down knowledge. Chapters cover topics such as the role of mentoring in spurring innovation and mentoring a diverse and dispersed workforce accustomed to interacting digitally. This hands-on guide teaches leaders to be the kind of confident coaches integral to learning organizations.

Print paperback, ISBN 978-1-60994-710-1
PDF ebook, ISBN 978-1-60994-711-8
ePub ebook, ISBN 978-1-60994-712-5

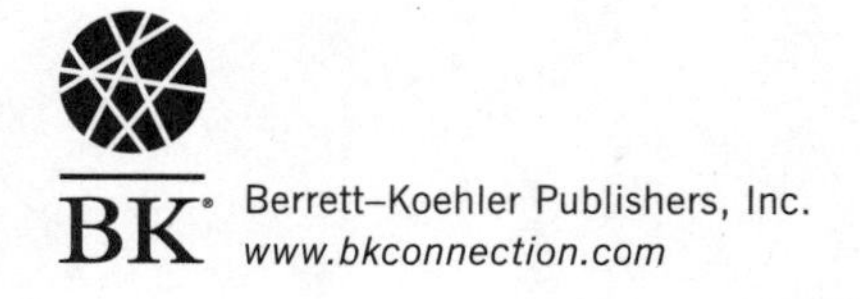

Berrett–Koehler Publishers, Inc.
www.bkconnection.com

800.929.2929

Berrett–Koehler
BK Publishers

Berrett-Koehler is an independent publisher dedicated to an ambitious mission: *Connecting people and ideas to create a world that works for all.*

Our publications span many formats, including print, digital, audio, and video. We also offer online resources, training, and gatherings. And we will continue expanding our products and services to advance our mission.

We believe that the solutions to the world's problems will come from all of us, working at all levels: in our society, in our organizations, and in our own lives. Our publications and resources offer pathways to creating a more just, equitable, and sustainable society. They help people make their organizations more humane, democratic, diverse, and effective (and we don't think there's any contradiction there). And they guide people in creating positive change in their own lives and aligning their personal practices with their aspirations for a better world.

And we strive to practice what we preach through what we call "The BK Way." At the core of this approach is *stewardship,* a deep sense of responsibility to administer the company for the benefit of all of our stakeholder groups, including authors, customers, employees, investors, service providers, sales partners, and the communities and environment around us. Everything we do is built around stewardship and our other core values of *quality, partnership, inclusion,* and *sustainability.*

This is why Berrett-Koehler is the first book publishing company to be both a B Corporation (a rigorous certification) and a benefit corporation (a for-profit legal status), which together require us to adhere to the highest standards for corporate, social, and environmental performance. And it is why we have instituted many pioneering practices (which you can learn about at www.bkconnection.com), including the Berrett-Koehler Constitution, the Bill of Rights and Responsibilities for BK Authors, and our unique Author Days.

We are grateful to our readers, authors, and other friends who are supporting our mission. We ask you to share with us examples of how BK publications and resources are making a difference in your lives, organizations, and communities at www.bkconnection.com/impact.

Dear reader,

Thank you for picking up this book and welcome to the worldwide BK community! You're joining a special group of people who have come together to create positive change in their lives, organizations, and communities.

What's BK all about?

Our mission is to connect people and ideas to create a world that works for all.

Why? Our communities, organizations, and lives get bogged down by old paradigms of self-interest, exclusion, hierarchy, and privilege. But we believe that can change. That's why we seek the leading experts on these challenges—and share their actionable ideas with you.

A welcome gift

To help you get started, we'd like to offer you a **free copy** of one of our bestselling ebooks:

www.bkconnection.com/welcome

When you claim your **free ebook**, you'll also be subscribed to our blog.

Our freshest insights

Access the best new tools and ideas for leaders at all levels on our blog at ideas.bkconnection.com.

Sincerely,

Your friends at Berrett-Koehler